Georgia Knights

Letters from a farmer to his sons

Barry Shinall

Georgia Knights

Letters from a farmer to his sons

Barry Shinall

Copyright © 2001
All Rights Reserved

PUBLISHED BY:
BRENTWOOD CHRISTIAN PRESS
4000 BEALLWOOD AVENUE
COLUMBUS, GEORGIA 31904

Dedication

Dedicated to my greatest achievement, my sons, Tom and Matt.

Acknowledgments

Thanks to my wife for her encouragement of this book, without her support it would never have been printed. To the best mom and dad a man could be blessed with, thanks for believing in me. To my sister for her editing, proofing, and suggestions, you're the best! And to my business and spiritual mentors, you know who you are, I love you dearly.

CONTENTS

Chapter   *Page*
1. WHO CARES? 5

2. WHO KNOWS? 22

3. WHO ARE YOU? 33

4. IN WHOM DO YOU BELIEVE? 49

5. WHAT HAPPENED? 65

6. ISN'T LIFE SWEET? 79

7. ARE YOU WILLING TO CHANGE? 95

8. WHAT'S NEXT? 113

EPILOGUE 119

Chapter 1
WHO CARES?

There is a saying that nobody cares how much you know until they know how much you care. How much truth in so few words!

We face a terrible problem in our world today and that is that our children see too many adults that don't care. We instill this in our preschool kids when we drop them off at a day care, pick them up and rush them to a sitter so mom and dad can have dinner alone. Our school age children are put in school systems that are overcrowded and many of the teachers consider their profession as "just a job." In college they are subjected to a whole new world of students who don't care about grades, going to class, or making a good impression. Then they enter the business world and it seems that no one cares about anything!

If you my children were to ask, "Dad why is it important to care?" I would tell you that first of all you should become caring individuals because in the course of your lives you will have an impact on many people, whether good or bad, some you will not even know. Second I want you to know that mom and dad care because you are a direct reflection of how we have raised you, and we want you to have a positive, motivated life. And most important that God cares, He loves each and everyone of us and desires the very best for us. If you adopt the attitude that everything you do is done to please God, then caring almost becomes an instinct.

MY BRIDE

As I write this letter I have just celebrated my twelfth wedding anniversary. As I sit and think of my wonderful wife, of all the dangers, toils and heartache that we've been through, I cannot help but marvel at how much I love your mother. I have heard others over the years talk about their marriage getting better but that was just so hard to believe. Now I can speak with authority that mine certainly has.

I remember so much about that day twelve years ago. You must realize that I had known Carolyn all my life, we had played together as children, had our first real date together, and generally just learned about life and growing up, together. My mother had told me that love was free; I found out otherwise. After my first date with your mother which included an afternoon matinee and popcorn, I had spent a whole five dollars! After a courtship of five years, at the tender age of twenty, we decided to live our lives together as man and wife.

A few days before our marriage a wise old man by the name of Mr. Baker, gave us some wonderful advise. Carolyn and I had gone for a Sunday afternoon walk and Mr. Baker was feeding his cows.

"You know," Mr. Baker said, "My wife and I have never had a fight in fifty years of marriage."

Seeing that I was somewhat skeptical he continued.

"It takes two people to fight. When she starts, I walk off. That's all there is to it."

It works!!

October 1, 1977, was a beautiful sunny morning with threatening clouds. The event was scheduled for 3:00 p.m. From lunch until 2:00 p.m. it poured, then the sun was out and a beautiful fall day began to unfold. The pastor was a great friend who had baptized me at the age of eight. My groomsmen consisted of two brothers-in-law, whom I hardly knew but would grow to love, a friend who a few years later I would be involved in a business venture with and another friend who later would be a big disappointment to me. Friends, even very good ones, will do that. And my best man was, of course, my dad who was then and still is my best friend. At the end of the ceremony we were officially man and wife, however, it has been our decision to stay married every day of our lives.

When you take your bride, I hope she's half the woman your mother is; if so, you've done a good day's work. Love is more than romance; it's loving her more than yourself. It is not jealous. It lets you plan your goals together as one. Giving 50/50 will not work, you must each give 100%.

We began a new life that day with no promises or guarantees, just hope and a lot of prayers. I will never forget the morning after our wedding night. I awoke with a wonderful new feeling. A feeling that never again will I have to face life alone, that never would I have to shoulder all the burdens, because now they could be divided by two. We were not married by accident or consequence, but with the intention of having a great life together.

My dad always told me that you never really know someone until you have worked with them or lived with them. He was right, but that's another story.

ANNIE

"Hello Barry, this is Sis." I heard your aunt's voice begin to break as she spoke over the phone. "Could you do me a big favor? Will you please let Annie come live with you in the country?" Belinda had a big black Labrador Retriever named Annie who was required to be chained in the city. It is my belief that nothing alive deserves to be chained, it's too harsh, too trapped. Annie, needless to say, hated it and barked all night long which made the neighbors very unhappy. Sis had a choice, give Annie to me or carry her to the pound.

"Sure hon, bring her over tomorrow." I was a farmer. I had plenty of mouths to feed and figured one more would not make much difference. And though I didn't know it at the time, I had just made one of the greatest decisions of my life.

It was late the next day when Belinda arrived with Annie. It was Spring and I had put in a full day's work; I almost dreaded having to "baby sit" a new animal. When Annie bounded out of the car I knew at once that she was home. She was built as only God builds Labradors: big, powerful, and full of energy. She was so black that she appeared blue, with a white diamond on her chest. She was about two years old. Her paws were perfectly webbed to allow her to swim the fastest and deepest waters. As Sis left, Annie was enjoying her first meal at home. I don't think she ever missed Sis, and she never barked at night again.

I spent most of the summer training Annie to fetch and not to fear guns. She was a natural born hunter and her instincts served her well. That fall we started hunting together and for many years thereafter we would both enjoy the sport. We hunted anything that could fly and to watch Annie retrieve was truly one of the joys of my life. She became my constant companion, spending the evening by my chair and jumping into the bed of the pickup anytime I went to the fields or to check livestock.

It was a beautiful summer day and I decided to walk down to the barn to check on the horses; Annie was right by my side. We had enjoyed a year together and we looked forward to our adventures on the farm, but neither was prepared for what happened that day. As I approached the barn Annie came to a halt, perked her ears, and tilted her head to one side. Not thinking much about it I thought she had discovered a mouse in the tall grass. Within seconds I heard the sound that will make any country boy shiver...RATTLER! Within a heartbeat she jumped on the big snake and in a whirlwind of barks and snarls she began to fight the adversary. My pleas for her to stop fell on deaf ears. Annie knew to stop or even slow down would make her an easy target for the striking serpent. After what seemed like a long time the old snake gave up and crawled off into the high grass. Annie had saved me from death or severe injury.

Annie had such a strange bark, "Awoo woo woo," it almost sounded like a siren. One morning I awoke to Annie's constant barking. I looked at my watch and it told me that it was two a.m. Dumb dog must have a opposum treed I thought. I stumbled to the back door and yelled for her to hush, but her bark was more persistent than ever. As I stepped off the porch I noticed that she was nearly in a point under our mobile home. I first thought that a varmint was under our home, but after an inspection I noticed steam coming from where the hot water heater was in our house. The heater had malfunctioned and the release valve would not open; within minutes our 12 x 70 home could be destroyed by the explosion! Without even calling your mother I ran to the power box to shut the power off. We waited in the yard until all the danger had passed, Carolyn, myself, and my dog.

I was in the pasture working one day when I realized I was being followed. We had a bull that was crazy and now he was stalking me as if I were his prey. Your father has never been a real bright person, but when the bull got within ten feet I turned and threw a hammer at him. The hammer hit its target right on the nose, boy was that a mistake! The 1200 pound bull became very angry, he shook his head and bellowed, he pawed the ground and lowered his head, his horns looked like lances and I knew he meant business. I looked to my left then to my right, and the closest fence was about 70ft to my left. I knew that I could never out run him and he knew I was scared. "Awoo woo woo!" Here came Annie! Up to the big bull she ran and bit him right on the nose, and that gave me the break I was looking for. I ran with all my might and scaled the barbed wire fence, right behind me was Annie who crawled under the fence and turned to face a foe that knew he had been defeated. Annie jumped and turned and barked, I thought I saw her smile, she had just got the best of an animal that outweighed her by over 1100 pounds. For the third time my friend had saved my life.

One day while cultivating soybeans I decided to drive my tractor home for lunch. Carolyn wasn't at home that day but I decided I would grab a quick sandwich before moving to another field. Upon entering the house I was horrified to find it ransacked. Someone had broken in and stolen all my guns and in the process turned the house inside out. I ran out the back door and to my disgust I saw Annie laying in a pool of blood. I'm sure she had valiantly tried to protect our home. The intruders had beaten her beyond belief and sprayed her eyes with windshield deicer. She was bleeding from her ears, eyes, nose, and mouth. From her breathing I knew she was hurt bad. The vet stood at the examining table and shook his head.

"Barry she has a broken hip, broken ribs, a severe concussion, and she is blind. Recovery will be long and hard, and she's not a young dog anymore. You must put her down."

Now it was my time to save her life. I told the vet to do whatever was necessary to save her life. For eight weeks I toted her in and out of the house. In time her bones healed, but she never hunted or swam again, but for many more years she loved me and I her.

Eleven years had past since Annie had came to live with us, but now the vet informed me that she had cancer and would never recover. Night after night I would lay in my bed and hear her moan from pain. Her food and water had to be brought to her. One morning before dawn I went out to the walk where she was laying and put her head in my lap, for hours I sat there stroking her head and she responded by wagging her old tail. "The time has come girl." I knew that I was making her suffer because of my selfishness. I know that only man has a soul and will have another life in Heaven above, therefore I knew as I left that morning that I would never see her again. Your mom agreed to take her to the vet, she knew it would be easier that way.

Later that morning Carolyn called to tell me it was over. I leaned over my desk and put my head in my hands. My throat tightened and my heart hurt, tears began to fall on my notepad. I couldn't believe I was crying over a dog. I was a farmer, I was use to death. On a farm you realize that everything must cycle, dying is just as natural as birth. But this death was different, none of those other animals were my friends.

I often take pleasure in remembering golden Fall afternoons with me and my gun, with Annie out front just waiting for me to bring down a fowl. I remember the cold winter nights by the fire and Annie by my chair. I remember watching her swim, she was so good at it. Boys I hope you will truly love a dog one day, the memories will last forever.

MY MENTOR

As I sit down to write about someone who has done so much I feel at loss for words. Every now and then someone comes into your life that will have a drastic affect on your character. Character is not an inheritance, each person must build it for himself. However I believe the Good Lord allows certain people to cross your paths that will become a teacher of character in your life.

The Summer of 1985 will always stand out in my mind as a time of great discontent. I had just went through a complete sell-out of my farm and other business interest. For the first time I was forced to seek employment off the farm. I had applied for the position of farm manager on Rollins Ranch, a three thousand acre horse farm. After days of interviews I was to finally meet the man who was to become my boss. Ken didn't impress me much that hot June afternoon, but as the years went by we would become friends in life, partners in business, and brothers in Christ.

Our tenure at Rollins only lasted about fifteen months and then we were off to bigger and better things. Ken taught me about so many different things, it is hard to point to any one thing as a highlight. He taught me everything I know about the business world, but mainly to seek God in all things that I do. I remember many times when we as partners faced business problems he would say, "Let's pray about it and God will let us know what to do." He taught me to have strength. One of his favorite sayings was, "Barry be bold, and mighty forces will come to your aid!" And he taught me how to have courage. He told me that it took a lot of courage to love and care for others.

Seeking Gods will for our lives seems like an easy concept, when in reality it is often hard to do. I knew that it was not God who created all the problems I faced on the farm, but as I sought His will for my life, I knew that His will was for me to sell everything I owned and start over. That was very hard to do. We are taught from birth to consult God on the life and death issues in life, but not to bother Him with the small things in life. Nothing could be further from the truth. As much as I love you, my sons, God loves you infinitely more. Just as I am interested in every decision that you make, your God is just as interested. If you learn to seek His guidance in all things, then Romans 8:28 will become alive in your life and the burdens of life will become lighter. Had I not followed Gods will and moved on, I might not have ever known Ken Morrow.

For we men, physical strength has always been an important part of our lives, but the real test of manhood is how tough you are mentally. We have a real man problem in our world today because too many men refuse to be strong mentally. It is our responsibility to be the financial supporters of our families as well as the spiritual leaders, in order to do this we must pray for strength to face each new day and each new problem. A woman likes nothing better than a man who knows where he is going, is committed to that goal, and knows how he's going to get there. Even though slaying the dragons of life is not fun, it is your responsibility as a man to do it.

I had become a person who didn't trust anyone, or want to help anyone before meeting Ken. I used the excuse that I had learned a lot about people from the business and political worlds and therefore wanted nothing to do with most folks. I submit to you that anyone with that attitude is a coward. You see it took great courage for the Good Samaritan to do what he did. Caring for someone isn't always pleasing, sometimes you will be hurt, other times you will suffer disappointment in your fellow man, but truly courageous men will put those thoughts aside in order to help others. Real men care about other peoples welfare, security, and souls.

As I write this letter my mentor continues to be a great source of leadership to me. Sometime, somewhere, a man will be provided, other than myself, to help you in your daily walk, I pray he's like Ken Morrow.

THE FIVE ASSETS OF LIFE

The other day I read an article by a local minister who said that he enjoyed his life more when he was broke and struggling than he does now that he is "comfortable." I find that hard to believe, your mom and I have been broke and we've had money. I must admit that having money is much better! Let me say this, many times in your life you will probably be broke, however I never want you to be poor. You see, "broke" is a temporary situation, "poor" is an attitude. Over the past several years I've had the opportunity to do a lot of speaking to all sorts of groups, from local civic groups to an association of retired people, from a group of pastors to a professional ball club, and many many more. I've shared this message with many people because there are five things that everybody, everywhere can use to their advantage. I can't guarantee success by using them, but I will guarantee that if you use them it will change your life.

What do you think about when the word "asset" is mentioned? If someone on the street was taking a survey and ask you to name your most valuable assets, what would they be? Your home? Your clothes? Maybe your furniture or your car? Those are the replies you would most likely get from the average person on the street. But when I think of my assets I don't think of material things first. I think of the love God has given me, and allows me to give to others. I think of my salvation through Jesus Christ, my wonderful loving family, my good health: mental, physical, and spiritual, and my wonderful wife that I share my life with.

But let's face it, everybody doesn't have good health, *or happy* close families, like I am blessed with, so I want to share with you five assets we all have access to. They are within our grasp if we want them.

The first is the ABILITY TO USE WHAT WE HAVE.

Remember the parable of the talents in Matthew 25: 14-30? A master gave one servant five talents, one servant two talents, and one servant one talent. After a period of time the master called his servants to see how they had used what they had been given. The first two servants had doubled their talents and were told that they had been faithful over a few things so they would be made rulers over many things. But the third servant was afraid of the challenge, he was afraid to take any risk with his talent, so he hid it. He buried it in the ground and did nothing with it. But his master was not pleased with what he had done, so he took his talent from him and gave it to one of the faithful servants. It is the same with us today. If we do not use what we have we will loose it. So we must cultivate the ability to use our talents.

The second asset is the SETTING OF GOALS.

So many times we limit ourselves unnecessarily. How excited I was when I discovered that I could have or do just about anything, just by setting a few goals. A trip around the world begins with one step. The setting of goals is very important. We must have something to work toward, something to challenge us. And regardless of what our goals may be, if we sincerely desire to achieve them and believe we can do it, then we can with Gods help. One of my favorite passages is Philippians 4:13, "I can do all things through Christ which strengthens me." Take note of the first seven words of that verse, and remember to write your goals down and put a realistic time in which you want to accomplish them. A goal without a time is only a wish.

The third asset is A POSITIVE SPIRIT

If you are not a Christian you may come up short on this one. As Christians we have the Holy Spirit with us twenty four hours a day, seven days a week. Romans chapter 8 deals with the spiritual life. Verse 9 says, "But ye are not in the flesh but in the spirit..." And 1 Corinthians 3:16 says, "Know ye not that we are the temple of God, and that the spirit of God dwelleth in you?" Our God is a loving God, He loved us so much that He gave us His only son, Jesus Christ to die for us. How could a loving God like that give us a negative and unhappy spirit by nature? He couldn't. If we as Christians are not positive then we have allowed Satan to get in between us and God. That my children is easy to happen.

The fourth asset is ENTHUSIASM.

Enthusiasm is inspiration or motivation, what makes us do things. There are different types of motivation.

1) Fear – We do something because we are afraid of what will happen if we don't. Like a donkey pulling a cart being whipped. This is a temporary motivation because it is external.

2) Reward – Our fringe benefits, or putting a carrot on a stick ahead of the donkey. This again is temporary because you begin to want larger benefits and fatter carrots.

3) Permanent – Comes from within and is based on your attitude. When someone ask the trainer why his thoroughbred race horse ran, the trainer replied, "Because he wants to."

MOTIVATION = GOAL + PLAN
We as Christians should compare ourselves with the thoroughbred race horse. We should want to inspire others. We should be a positive, motivating force, not only for ourselves, but for others as well. In Luke chapter 8 Jesus cast the devils out of the man from Gadara, Jesus told him to return to his home and show of the things God had done for him. Not only did he go home, he went to the whole city!
He was excited, inspired, motivated, and enthusiastic! Are we very enthusiastic about anything today?
The last asset is *FAITH*.
Faith pulls all the other assets together. How important is faith? Well the Bible talks more about faith than it does heaven. Hebrews chapter 11 tells us what faith is. Matthew 17:20 tells us that, "If ye have the faith as a grain of mustard seed...nothing shall be impossible unto you." Mark 9:23 says, "If thou canst believe, all things are possible to him that believeth." We must have faith. It takes faith to believe in a promise made by Jesus in Matthew 28:20, "...and, lo I am with you alway, even until the end of the world."
Examine your lives my sons. Can you claim all five of the assets on your spiritual financial statement? If not do whatever is necessary to reclaim your assets of life. Do not allow your life to become as the mans whose epitaph read, "He ask little of life, and life paid his price."

GEORGIA
I saw a bumper sticker the other day that read: "American by birth, Southern by the grace of God!" Boy did I like that sticker! It sums up the way I feel, not only about the South, but about our state. For a long time I thought that my love affair with Georgia was not natural,

but later I realized that what I feel is a great sense of pride in a state that is truly great.

In 1982 I ran for the House Of Representatives (I lost), not so much for ego, power, or prestige, but just to be a part of the history of this state. The history in our home state is very rich; one of the original colonies, cultural home of the Cherokee Indians, and rising back from the ashes that Sherman's army left behind. We are proud that we had a president from Georgia, and that many of our citizens helped design the Civil Rights bill that changed the free world.

Our climate is perfect, we have absolutely beautiful Springs which are full of splendid dogwood blooms, our Summers are hot and humid with cool pleasant evenings. The Fall in Georgia brings people from near and far to see our beautiful foliage, and the winters are cool but never very cold.

Two of the things we are best known for is food and our hospitality. Fried Chicken, green beans, corn on the cob, fried okra, cornbread, iced tea (very sweet), pecan pie with home made vanilla ice cream is as common in Georgia as hot dogs are in Chicago. Southern hospitality is not something that can be taught, it must be caught. I once heard a man reply that wealth and riches were of no value if you didn't have hospitality. Here in Georgia we take manners very seriously, not to ask about the health of another's mamma and daddy is considered very rude.

Our geography is unlike any other in the Union. The mountains in Northeast Georgia are part of the Appalachian chain, the Appalachian trail ends here (or begins, depending upon if you are coming or going). Small mountain towns such as Dallonega, Dawsonville, and Blairsville come alive with Fall festivals. With majestic views and sparkling waterfalls the Georgia mountains are breathtaking. Georgia is blessed with a beautiful coastline, that boast a fine sampling of island flavor. The Golden Isles and historic Savannah are among my favorite places in the world. In Southern Georgia you can raise or grow just about anything, this provides for a tremendous diversity base for area farmers. To speak of Georgia and not mention Atlanta would be a shame. Atlanta is one of the truly great cities of the world, with fine restaurants, professional sports, and lots of hospitality.

This is not a letter for a tourism add, however it is a recommendation. Your dad is very proud of this state. I care for Georgia and her future. I hope you my sons will consider Georgia the brightest star in the Southern sky.

A GLITTERING BODY OF WATER

It was a beautiful Fall afternoon 1982. The sun reflected off of a perfectly calm lake, the weather was hot. We were fishing just east of Bill's boat dock on Lake Allatoona, not having a lot of luck, but having a great time. Chirl and I were fishing buddies, sure he was my father-in-law, your grandfather, a very good friend, but nothing compares to the bond that is formed between fishing buddies. As we sat on the bank laughing and having fun his conversation turned serious, he told me that he was having problems swallowing, that he felt as if he had a "peanut husk" in his throat. I told him not to worry about it, soon it would probably go away. Little did I know at the time that this was probably the beginning of the end for your grandfather.

How can I put into words how much I cared for Chirl, or how much that I still care for him, several years after his death. He succumbed to cancer a year and a half after that Fall day in 1982. Tom, you were still a very small baby at the time of his death, he called you "his little angel." I believe you will inherit his love for fishing. Matt, you were named after your grandfather whose full name was Madison Chirl Abernathy. Every time I look at you I think of him, you have his personality. Chirl (pronounced curl) had a fantastic personality, he was always laughing and having fun, he was very jolly. When he did loose his temper he got over it quick.

You must realize that I loved Chirl before I loved your mother, he and I were fishing buddies before I started dating Carolyn. During the fifteen or so years that I knew him we fished in ponds, rivers, lakes, and streams. We fished in hot dry weather and cold rainy days. We fished in the morning, afternoon, and night, windy or calm. We had good days and bad, caught big-ones and lost big-ones. We enjoyed eating our catch, any given weekend you could find Chirl cooking fried fish, hushpuppies, cole slaw, rolls, french fries, onion rings, and wash it down with ice cold coke.

Chirl was a welder by trade and often came to my rescue on the farm when machinery broke down. Of all the things he taught me, I think the greatest thing he possessed was showing people that he really and truly cared for them. I remember one trip to the lake when we stopped at the bait shop for minnows. A young couple with a baby was asking the store owner for credit to buy food, The store owner, although very polite, refused saying that it was against his policy. Seeing the situation Chirl took every penny he had and gave it to the couple, the girl cried and the husband accepted it with heartfelt thanks. We had no money for bait so we returned home realizing that on that day we had been fishers of men. One of the basic desires of human beings is to feel loved and cared for, but unfortunately we fail to show or tell others. Chirl had a great way of letting others know of their value in his eyes. We should never be afraid to let others know how much we love and admire them. I can never remember Chirl criticizing me for anything, he realized that if you ever hurt someone else's feelings that you also diminish their ability to live life to its fullest. If a person's self confidence remains high they will be able to accomplish almost anything.

On that faithful Fall afternoon your grandfather said something to me I shall never forget, "Barry if I should die before you, I want you to think of me anytime you see a glittering body of water. After all that's where I will be. I'll be fishing with Peter and all the other fishermen." I never wet a hook that I don't think of that evening, I feel as though he really is with me. As the sun began to set and cast a red glow on the glass like lake, we packed up and headed home never to fish again.

Chapter 2
WHO KNOWS?

The great scientist Albert Einstein once wrote, "Imagination is more important than information." How important is all the "stuff" we learn in life? You will hear people who express the belief that education is the most important thing in the world, yet so many of the great people that have left their mark on this world have never had much public education. There are those who believe that desire and attitude will get you to where you want to go, but the cemeteries are full of people who had a gut burning hunger to succeed, a marvelous positive attitude, yet died broke. And then you will have those who believe all one needs is good common sense, however most of the mules I ever met had common sense.

In 1 Kings chapter 3, the young king Solomon had a dream, in this dream God ask him what he wanted most in life. The young boy king asked for wisdom so that he could become an effective leader. God was pleased with Solomon and granted him an understanding heart, as you know Solomon became the richest man in the world, a great ruler, and all he desired was wisdom.

It is my prayer for you boys to take advantage of all the above. You see in this life you will be on a continuous learning experience. The public education you receive will take many years, and what you learn in school will not make you successful, but you will use it everyday of your life. You need to dream big dreams and have a positive outlook on life, you need to be open minded. Common sense can not be taught, it must be sought. Let me encourage you to pray daily for wisdom for it does come from God.

Charlie "Tremendous" Jones says that you will be the same person five years from today except for the people you meet and the books you read. That places an enormous value on the daily events in life and the people we associate with. As you travel through life you will have great opportunities to learn. You will be affected by many of the people in your lives, please try to learn from every individual. When you travel, learn about the places you see. Take the advice of reading seriously, don't read useless junk, but expand your reading habits to a broad range of subjects. The following are a few lessons that I have learned, they may come in handy one day.

MR. PRESIDENT

The world was young and so was I. Life was full of adventures and everyday I looked forward to the next. I was facing my first real farm crisis, the drought had taken its toll and many of the area farmers had gathered at a local auditorium to discuss the seriousness of the hour. I felt that I could withstand the initial loss but many of the farmers were facing some hard financial situations. After hours of heated debate it was decided that a delegation should be sent to Washington D.C. and let them know first hand of our problems. The motions were made, three men would go, and your dad was one of them! Few times in my life have I ever been that excited! This was my chance to make a difference, an opportunity to prove my stuff. And so my political interest started that Fall afternoon in Cartersville, Georgia.

It was now early February and the time for the great mission was upon us, the arrangements had been made, an itinerary for three days had been set up to let us speak to many key officials. I was excited about my first airline flight and many friends and family members wished us luck as we departed. As I settled into my plane seat I began to think of all the things that lay before me. One of my biggest problems was to try to decide about my future, I had been offered a great job off the farm, but my heart yearned to stay and build a profitable operation. Your mother and I were still newlyweds and I was farming a very small amount of land. I had been praying for an answer, I needed to let the employer know something. What should I do? Life seems to get awful complicated after you pass eighteen.

The weather in Washington was typical for February, cold, snowy, and wet. Our mission was simple but very important, let our legislators know that we needed emergency farm loans at low interest to put in a crop that Spring. I was so excited to be in the city where all the world watches to see what happens next.

The first two days had flown by in a flurry of meetings with Congressmen, Senators, and members of the U.S.D.A. Our nights were spent at great restaurants pouring over the volumes of information we were receiving. Our last day was free except for a late four p.m. meeting at the White House with an aide to the president. That day was very cold and overcast, the air filled with a freezing rain. We spent hours in the Smithsonian Institute investigating the wonders of the world, there was the remains of a dinosaur, we stood staring at the first airplane that was flown by the Wright brothers, and we were told that they had a real moon rock on display. And even though I was beyond myself with enthusiasm, I still was burdened over my future. "Oh God," I would silently pray, "can't You give me a yes or no answer?"

We began our journey to the White House, and I still remember that we got lost on Pennsylvania Avenue. The last two days had been a tremendous boost for my confidence, but when the guard led us to the offices of the White House I begin to tremble at the thought of walking those hallowed halls. Here history had been shaped, presidents had walked these very halls, tears came to my eyes as I saw portraits of a few men that had called this house home. A receptionist showed us to a room and remarked that someone would be with us shortly. The room was beautiful, lots of hand rubbed wood, a crackling fire in a marble fireplace, leather furniture, and a faint but distinct odor of numerous fine cigars that had been smoked in the past. I looked at my watch, four p.m. A representative should be here soon.

"Good Day," he said as he entered the room, we immediately shot to our feet. All of my confidence was gone, my knees trembled, my heart raced. Before me stood the President of the United States, Jimmy Carter.

He wore a tie but instead of a coat he had a sweater on, it made him look like a real person. He was wearing the Carter smile that he had become famous for. As he shook our hands he made us feel at home and he was pleased that we had visited. He told us that having been a farmer from Georgia himself, he wanted to meet with us personally. Soon we were all talking as if we were neighbors, discussing crop problems, people we knew, and our faith in God. He began to expound on the many problems facing the free world, he got up and walked over to the fire, giving it a stoke. "You know," he said, "many times I pray and ask God what I should do next." Immediately I thought of my own problem, maybe it wasn't as important as world affairs, but it was something that I needed an answer for. Forgetting my nervousness I ask, "Mr. President, what if you hear no answer from God?" He looked at me very seriously then grinned, "Then the answer is no. You see God expects us to create a few opportunities of our own." He walked back to his chair and leaned forward, "He always answers, we just have to be sensitive to His will." Our meeting continued for the remainder of the hour, he promised his help with our problem, and said he would be praying for us. "Ya'll come back now!" He waved as he left the room.

We came back home with the feeling that our mission was successful (we did receive federal aide that Spring). But more important to me was that my question had been answered, I remained on the farm and expanded my operation greatly over the next few years. Still to this day I remember the lesson that I learned from a president, if your prayers seem unanswered maybe they already have been. We must create many of our own opportunities. I doubt if Mr. Carter even remembers that afternoon, but his remarks made a definite impact on my life.

THE IF IDA'S

One must always be careful of this dangerous and contagious disease, the "If Ida's." It creates within ones self a sort of self-centeredness that can be fatal if left untreated. You can see this at any farm supply dealership or local coffee shop – the "If Ida's."

"If Ida" only bought that peace of land over there, I'd be rich today!

"If Ida" invested in Chrysler stock!

"If Ida" started my business when you did!

"If Ida" worked harder!

"If Ida" married someone rich!

What a tremendous waste of time, but you hear it everyday and if you are not careful you will use it yourself and not even know it. To focus on what might have been is to lie and wallow in your past mistakes. Also notice in this form of complaining that you are always drawing attention to yourself, you are at center stage. The "If Ida's" will serve only to depress you and accomplish very little else. Someone once wrote that we can never predict our own thoughts, but we are always sure that disappointment will last forever.

One thing that I want you boys to always remember is that you can't climb the ladder of success with your hands in your pockets. You must always be reaching upward for the next rung, don't let the "If Ida's" cause you to loose valuable time looking back, when you need to be looking forward toward your goals.

Thomas Carlyle wrote a saying that we all should pay careful attention to, he states that people who would never think of committing suicide or ending their lives, would think nothing of dribbling away minutes and hours everyday. Boys you can forget your mistakes if you remember their lessons. The best way that I know of to become an old dog is to quit learning new tricks. The best cure for the "If Ida's" is to develop the attitude that never again will you wait for opportunity to knock. If it is meant to be, it is up to me!

The real sad note to the "If Ida's" is when there is nothing you can do about them, I heard a pastor the other day talking about his dad. He had been a bad provider for the family, he gambled, he drank, this caused his son to reject him. Resentment grew until after the fathers death, then the preacher felt a tremendous amount of loss and grief. He had never in his adult life told his dad that he loved him.

"If Ida" only told him once that I loved him, my life would be better today."

As I close I have one quotation more that I would like to share with you;

> It is impossible to become educated by learning only what we like.
>
> by Dr. Frank Crane

THE DREAMER

As far as I was concerned my life had come to an end. I had been farming for ten years under the idea that bigger was better, I found out that bigger meant that I could loose more money. Like thousands of other farmers across America I faced loosing everything that I had ever worked for. During the long hot summer of 1984 a man came into my life that taught me the importance of dreams. Tommy and I had become business partners that year in a marketing business. One day he remarked to me that my biggest problem was that I had quit dreaming.

He was right, all my dreams had become nightmares, while most people dream of getting ahead, my dream was to get back to even. Tommy taught me that without dreaming you could never become successful. Dreams are the fuel for the achievers of this world. Dreams give you more energy, they help you overcome your fears, it gives you a clear focus on where you are going. Tommy would spend hours telling me about his dreams, of a new luxury car, an airplane, of a beautiful dream home, for the freedom to hunt and fish wherever and whenever he wanted, (just to let you know, all those dreams did become reality), but he also helped me to develop my own. At first all I wanted was to get out of debt, but as time went by I began to realize how important it was to dream.

Ben Franklin once wrote, "Dead at age twenty-one. Buried at age sixty-five. The average American." Sadly enough there are many today who are already dead because they will not allow themselves to dream.

One of my big concerns was that as a Christian I didn't know if I should dream. Nothing could be farther from the truth! Our Father in Heaven already owns everything! He wants us to desire better things for our lives and our families.

Many people associate dreaming with fantasizing. The big difference between the two is that a dream is something that motivates you, it's something that you are willing to work and sacrifice for. A fantasy on the other hand is a mere visualization of something pleasing to you, they are simply a way of passing time. Volumes have been written about the importance of a vision, but I think it is neat that God would send a man into my life to teach me this principle.

As you boys go through your lives you will undoubtedly have some failures, it will become easy to get discouraged, that's when your dreams will come to your rescue. Everybody has their own dreams, it is important that you develop your dreams and not let anyone else steal it from you. Tommy's lesson to me: "No one who has ever achieved, did so without first dreaming about it."

THE KEYS TO SUCCESS

The year and a half that I spent as farm manager on one of the largest ranches in Georgia was time that God used to heal some very sore wounds. I had just lost the farming operation that had been in my family for generations, the men before me had been through the settling of a wild frontier inhabited by Indians. They had endured a Civil war and two World wars, not to mention the great depression.

The guilt of failure rode heavily on my shoulders. Decisions, regardless of how small, were difficult for me to make. My business skills had been dulled and I honestly wondered if I would ever be successful. I began a slow process of recovery on this large North Georgia horse farm, hours of peace and quiet and any major decisions had to be made by someone else. Although I didn't particularly like the job, it provided much needed opportunities for me to expand my abilities.

The youngest owner of the ranch seemed to come up more often than the rest, that was fine with me, I liked him more than the others. He always made me feel that I was an important part of the farm. He very seldom criticized, and had a way of making suggestions that made you feel like he was consulting you. He was more human than the other members of the family, you must realize these people were among the super rich. One Fall weekend he came up with his kids for a weekend of camping and fun. Everything was prepared but he always wanted me to accompany him while out exploring the vast acreage. On this particular Saturday afternoon we decided to have lunch at a local fast food restaurant. As we sat and enjoyed our meal of cheeseburgers and fries, I realized that I was in the presence of one of the richest men in the world, what a opportunity to pick his brain! I had only one question, what does it take to become successful? Instead of answering me with a bunch of philosophical mumbo-jumbo he gave me several things that he thought was essential for success in virtually anything you do. I committed them to memory and now I will write them down for you, someday you will realize the importance of each one.

#1 Associate with people who are achievers. They don't have to be in the same field as you, as long as they are suc-

cessful. One of the first lessons we learn from our parents is not to hang around with the wrong crowd, well the same principle can be applied to associating with winners. You can't soar with the eagles if you scratch with the turkeys. He told me that if he were totally broke he would do whatever was necessary to be around successful people, if only for a few minutes a day.

#2 *Read positive, motivational books.* All reading is fundamental. A person needs to develop the habit of reading. It doesn't matter if you like to read or not, if you want to succeed you must. A person must make reading a part of his daily schedule. Remember gossip magazines and romance novels are trash, trash in – trash out.

#3 *Listen to cassette tapes.* One of the least used tools is the tape player. While going down the road you can have the advice of a successful business person right there in the car with you. You can listen to motivational speakers at only a fraction of what it would cost to see them live. Complete education seminars can be taught on tape.

#4 *Don't make snap decisions.* Hollywood has glamorized powerful people making an instant decision without much thought. This action will almost always end in disaster. Any decision should be considered, put aside, and then reconsidered later. It never hurts to sleep (maybe several nights) on a business deal. Never buy something or invest in something until you think and pray about it for several days. A good rule of thumb: If it looks good today, it will look good next week. When someone tells you, "this deal won't last!" They are probably right-stay away!

#5 *Attend continuing education seminars.* Anytime you have the opportunity to learn more about your specific interest you need to. Often these seminars are very inexpensive and very informative. Conventions, trade shows, and rallies are essential learning tools. Medicine might never have made the great strides it has had it not been for continuing education seminars. These events will also let you associate with others that share common goals.

#6 Be Your own boss. How difficult it must have been for my boss to tell his own employee this. You will never be paid what you are worth as long as you work for someone else. Why make someone else successful instead of yourself. The best boss I ever had was me! My wife sleeps with the boss! The most sure way of arriving is to get others to duplicate you.

Over the years I have studied these keys and found them to be invaluable. If you boys will commit these to memory the long road of life may not be so bumpy.

Chapter 3
WHO ARE YOU?

One of the greatest tragedies of all human experience is to go through life and at life's end not know who you are. Our lives are full of events, people, and places that help develop who we really are. Unfortunately many people will live a whole life never coming to terms with what they really feel, what they believe in, or worse of all trying to live the life they think others would live.

As you fella's grow older you will undoubtedly have some success as well as failures, how you handle both will tell you a lot about yourselves. You will come in contact with many people whom you can impersonate but you must develop a feeling for being your own man. As you travel from farm life to great cities, lifestyles will also change, but if you hold onto your proud rural heritage, in the end the results will be easier to swallow.

I think the key word here is honest. One must learn how to be honest with themselves. This is a tough situation. It is often scary. Honestly facing your problem will mean that you don't have to pretend that you are somebody you're not. This doesn't mean that you have to be completely satisfied with every aspect of you life, but if you have guts enough to accept who you are and make the commitment to do whatever is necessary to pull out of it, you can make it from there. If you are honest about your life you can quit trying to fool your friends, your family, and most of all yourself. If you are honest with yourself your burdens will be lighter and you can enthusiastically chase life.

One important lesson that I have learned is that there is no inferior or superior people. You don't have to impress anyone by pretending to be something your not. I hope you boys will always be able to look in the mirror and recognize the person looking back.

THIS TOO SHALL PASS

What a wonderful year 1975 had been. I had graduated from high school, your mother and I were very much in love and saw each other daily, and I had become a full partner with an uncle on our 60 acre cotton farm. Oh I had planted a few acres on my own before, but this year had been special, I felt as though my career was being launched. My days were full of farm activities that I loved, I had worked the summer as a cotton insect scout for the extension service and had made some really good money, but our crops were superb and a bumper crop was forecast.

October 8th was a beautiful day. The fall weather in North Georgia had been fantastic. The sun shone warm, the trees were a grand array of colors, my flannel shirt felt good as I went about my daily chores on my beloved farm.

We had planted about two acres of peas on some new ground that year and had a bountiful harvest all summer, that afternoon my uncle, dad, and myself decided to gather some dried peas for winter use. After gathering several bushels and placing them on the back of our one ton truck we decided to inspect the cotton crop one more time. As we walked to the edge of a thirty acre field the cotton was about chest high and loaded with bolls from top to bottom, about 50% of the bolls were opened and we figured we could start picking as early as next week. Dad remarked that he wished he had 200 acres just like this, and my uncle believed we could pick an average of 2 bales per acre. Dad looked at his watch, 5pm, we needed to get back to the house, supper would be ready soon.

October 9th began as another beautiful fall day. The weather report that morning said that a Hurricane named "Eloise" was due for landfall any minute in the Gulf and this would bring us rain for the next several days, just as well I thought, this will give us time to get the cotton picker ready for harvest. That morning my uncle and I completed several chores just before the skies turned gray and began to sprinkle. He decided we should call it a day and get started on the picker first thing in the morning. I spent the dreary afternoon studying an electronics course at my desk. Mother came to my room and ask me to come look at the Western sky, she said it was an unusual color. I knew immediately we were in for bad weather, the air was still and humid, the skies black and in the west was an eerie yellow cloud which nearly always meant hail.

Eloise struck North Georgia with tremendous force. For over an hour we had winds of 70mph, the ground was completely covered with hail, the rain came down in torrents. Mother and I were at home alone and while mother feared for our safety, and for dad's who was on his way home, my worries focused only on my crop. No one will ever understand the love affair a farmer has with his crops. He gives them conception as he places the seed in the warm earth, he holds his breath till he sees little shoots of green coming up. He carefully cultivates the crop putting just the right amount of dirt around the small plants. All summer he will do battle with weeds and insects to insure the safety of his maturing plants. And then, as I had done the day before, he can stand proudly looking over his fields and feel a tremendous sense of pride and accomplishment. A farmer truly loves his crops because in a strange way they are a part of him.

As the storm subsided we hurried to the same thirty acre field to see what damage had been done. Mom, dad, my aunt, my uncle, and myself stood in complete silence as we gazed at a field that had been completely stripped of its crop. At that moment I felt for the first time a sudden jolt in my knowledge of life. Everything seemed utterly hopeless, my knees were weak and I wondered if this was what dying felt like. No one talked, I was glad that it was raining, maybe my family could not see my tears and know I was crying.

As the thunder rolled in the Eastern sky I hoped they could not hear my heart breaking. Right now my family needed me to be strong, they needed a hero, but for the life of me I felt as though I had just lost a friend. I looked at my watch, 5pm, what a difference a day can make!

For the next several days we all went around in a daze. Lots of work had to be done. Our homes and barns needed repairs, many trees had to be cut up, but that empty feeling of no crop to harvest was more than I could stand. I pleaded with God for help, I was so thankful that we were all uninjured, but yet my life was suddenly very stale and flat. I went out to the edge of the field one night after supper, the night was dark, but clear. The air smelled so fresh as it often does after a storm. I stood there and listened, nothing, no noise, everything quiet. I really don't know what I was expecting to hear but I knew that God and I needed to converse. I sat down on the damp earth, the temperature was cool. I closed my eyes and began to see the beautiful crop as it had been. I began to see all the other crops in my life, some from many years earlier. It seemed to make me feel better to remember the good harvest of the past. I could smell the cotton as it was being picked, I could hear the rustle of dried stalks, I could see the sun setting with an orange glow as equipment was being shut down for the night. And then it hit me, there will be other crops to harvest! Sure this year was gone, but next year I know we will have a good harvest! And then out of my mouth came the words I needed so bad, "This too shall pass."

As you boys grow older try to keep in your mind that this too shall pass. When your down, when you feel alone, when your desperate, when your heart breaks, always remember: This too shall pass.

PETE

July 1,1985 I started my new job as farm manager for Rollins Ranch in Cartersville. My mission there was a complicated one, the farm itself consisted of about 3500 acres that had to be cleared, pastured, and fenced. There were barns to be built, ponds to be dammed. The biggest chore at hand was to build a large 80-100 acre lake, which meant lots and lots of land clearing.

One of my first duties was to hire my crew. I have always taken this responsibility seriously. My philosophy is that it is bad enough to have to work, so you might as well surround yourself with people that you enjoy being with. Pete was a young man at the time fresh out of school, he called me one night and ask for a job. My initial reaction was that he was too young and had no experience, fortunately I was able to tell him that I didn't need anyone and that I appreciated him calling. Well the next afternoon Pete shows up at my house with a very short resume' and a desire to work on a real horse farm, still I told him that all positions were full. I told your mother that night that I had never seen someone so anxious to work. The next night he called again, and again I found myself apologizing because

I really couldn't use him. The next morning was Thursday and one of my employees showed up drunk, this is something that I have never tolerated and fired him on the spot. The first person that I thought of was Pete. Friday morning at 7am he was at work, and so began a relationship that was much more than employer and an employee.

As time went by I found Pete to have an outstanding attitude toward work, he would attack any job regardless of size, and he would seize any opportunity to learn anything new. I found myself liking Pete more and more. He learned to operate any piece of equipment on the farm and as he matured I found myself putting more and more responsibilities on his young shoulders. He told me onetime his secret for tackling any situation, "When I have a job that I don't like I feel that I have three choices, first I could complain and dread it, second I could grit my teeth and endure it, or third I can just go ahead and do it and get it over with," After that I felt as though young Pete had grasp a truth that many will never know about. The time passed quickly and soon over a year had gone by, time had come to clear the lake bed.

August of 1986 was a scorcher, many days were over 100 degrees and the air always seemed heavy with humidity. The loggers had finished their job on the lake bed and now we had to pile hundreds of brush piles, burn them, then bury the remains. On the tenth day of that month Pete was in the valley running a backhoe burying stumps while I torched piles of debris. At 4:30pm I had just thrown some brush on an unlit pile when Pete drove up on the tractor, although it was nearly time to leave I decided that I would light one more fire and told Pete he could go ahead and go in, instead he opted to stay with me, little did we know that both of our lives was fixing to change. I tried to pump up a sprayer with fuel to spray on the green brush, but the sprayer was so low on fuel I had to release the pressure and pour what little fuel there was out on the limbs. As I struck my lighter the fumes around me literally exploded, I was on fire!

I had always been told to lay down and roll to smother the fire, well my mind knew that but my feet didn't. I looked down and saw that my right arm and my left hand was on fire, I slapped at my face to try and stop the intense heat, and realized that I was only raking off skin, I panicked, I ran. The next thing I knew Pete had chased me down, tackled me and started throwing dirt all over me. Pete weighed about 145 pounds I was well over 250 pounds, yet he drug me to the pickup and somehow put me in. As I traveled to the hospital I kept my mind off the pain by reciting a prayer by Reinhold Niebuhr, "Oh Lord, grant me the strength to change things that need changing, the courage to accept things that can not be changed, and the wisdom to know the difference." Once in the hospital I found out that I could still see and although I had been badly burned it could have been much worse, if not for Pete I would be an ash heap in that lake bed.

AS I laid in intensive care I found out a few things about myself, I had always wondered how I would handle a major accident, and I was proud of myself for remaining in a prayerful attitude during the whole ordeal. I also found out that after becoming a lit torch I ran, I will never know why. But my mind kept returning to Pete time and again, I looked forward to thanking him personally and promised myself I would see to it that he got a raise.

The next day Pete came to visit me. In his usual humble manner he swore that anybody would have done what he did and proceeded to tell me he would take over all management responsibilities while I recovered. I ask him why he risk his own life, why he didn't panic. "Well, he said, I knew I didn't have till next week to make a decision." I ask him where did he find the courage to tackle a man on fire, especially when he outweighed him by 100 pounds? "It was difficult, very difficult. But I knew that I would have to live with myself and my decision forever. I chose to take the chance."

I believed that Pete learned a few things about himself that hot summer day. I know that he gave me the opportunity to stay around and raise you boys, I also know that he has the stuff that all men want, but may never know they have.

THE DAY WE FAILED

I write this letter to you Tom, because we had a conversation the other night that I don't believe a six year old can fully grasp. I was shaving, getting ready to go to a meeting after I had already put in a nine hour day at the office. You came into the bathroom and stood there looking up at your dad. When I ask what was on your mind, you ask a question that I'm sure you had put an awful lot of thought into. "Dad, when are we going to be rich?" Somewhat surprised I took you aside and told you the following story, I decided to put it in print because years from now it might come in handy for you.

I told you that some day we would be rich, or at least richer than we are now. Daddy has some well defined goals, I have a game plan, and we are working steadily toward where we want to be. Then I ask you a question, "Son, do you remember the day we failed?" You looked at me with those big blue eyes and shook your head no. "You see son the reason you can't remember is that it didn't happen on any one particular day, yet it was a progression of mistakes made over a period of years. Our success will occur the same way, it will take goals, plans, and lots of work for us to eventually become the successful people we dream of." When I ask if you understood, you nodded and ran off to play a game of adventure with your brother. You may not have understood anything that I said, but it caused your old man to ponder on the answer. Although I gave you a wonderful answer, it is a concept that many will never put to use

It has been said that people will spend more time planning a vacation than they do planning their future. I agree totally with that statement. I know because I suffered from the same stupidity for years. Most people are too busy making a living to make any money. Many people believe that the price of success is too high, well the other night I was coming home from a business meeting, it was late and I was bone tired. Why in the world am I doing this? I thought to myself. Then the realization struck me. The price of success only has to be paid one time, but the price for failure you pay for everyday. Every time you go to a job you dislike you are paying the price of failure. Every time a creditor calls and hounds you, you are paying the price of failure. Every time you go to the mailbox and pick up a stack of bills you can't pay, you are paying the price of failure.

During the farm crisis of 1984 I found myself facing a quarter of a million dollars of debt, two attorneys suggested that I file bankruptcy, but I decided that I had dug the hole over a period of many years and that someday, somehow I would just have to fill it up. My first item of business was to change. You see many people will go right on failing because they are afraid to change. I decided to sell everything that your mother and I owned to try to get out of debt. We sold four businesses, our home, our land, automobiles, even guns I no longer could afford shells for. After all that we found ourselves without jobs and still $31,000 in debt! We started over with you, a dog, and an old pickup that was soon to be reposed, but we had made the decision to change, and once you make a decision a way will provide itself.

Next we wrote down some personal as well as business goals we wanted to reach. We dared ourselves to dream bigger than ever and we began to visualize what we wanted. Visualization is far more than imagination. It always gives you a dimension of reality. All inventions are brought about by the inventor first visualizing them. And to go along with these original goals we outlined some simple, basic steps that we felt like would get us closer to our dreams. These are things you must do in order to get on the road to success. No, it is not easy at first. But the unfolding of these events, taken step by step will give you the solid foundation needed by successful people. Just always remember, inch by inch it's a sinch. Yard by yard it's hard.

The human body is a fantastic machine capable of solving the most tremendous of problems. At the time of this writing your mother and I are far from being rich. But looking back, we are nearly debt free, your mother doesn't have to work, and many other goals are coming to pass. We are following our plans and our destination is in sight. Yes son we will be rich Thursday...maybe not this Thursday or next, but one Thursday we will be, and then we will probably realize that the adventure isn't the success, but rather found along the journey to success.

I.S.I.

Inadequate Self Image, for brevity sake I will refer to it as I.S.I. This is something that most people in the world have and yet seldom ever admit it. After having to sell my farm, business ventures, and personal belongings I began for the first time in my life to have some serious doubts about myself. No longer could I feel secure in any decision I made, I had no confidence in myself, the simplest decision would strike fear into my heart. I stopped going to any social functions because I knew everyone there would be discussing my problems, I resigned from the board of directors of a local industry because of my "imagined inadequacies," my emotions were a mess, and I could not love myself. We are told in the Bible that we are to love our neighbors as ourselves, but that's hard to do when you dislike yourself. After time and a lot of self discipline, I began to regain my confidence but I still wondered if others suffered from the same problems I had experienced. I decided to do some research of my own, so I began to ask some respected friends, (whom I thought very successful), if they had ever suffered from I.S.I. and did they know why?

My first stop was to the pastor of a local church who had his doctorate in Theology and had published some writings. After posing the question to him he leaned back in his chair and formed a tent with his fingers. "Barry we all suffer from I.S.I. to some degree, it is one of the first things formed in our lives. As children we start developing our own inadequacies whether real or created. Take the child for example that sees his dad doing chores around the house, after watching his hero for a few minutes he ask his dad if he can help, dads reaction will help determine how this child will see himself. If dad gives the child some small task, regardless of how simple, the boy will be satisfied and pleased. If dad then praises his son it gives his self image a lift and will generate a creative habit. But consider if dad tells him no, that he can not do the work. The child, still curious and wants desperately to learn so he can help, but now dad gets mad at the child's persistence, he screams at the boy and maybe even punishes him for what the father feels is a deliberate disobedience, this reaction will start an I.S.I. pattern that will hinder his effectiveness forever."

"Can such small everyday occurrences really effect our lives even as adults?" I ask.

With a more serious look than before he replied, "These so called small things will probably be a major factor in our success or failure, they may even help form our destiny."

Next I traveled to Middle Georgia to talk to a man who had been my friend for years. He had also had some rough times, he had farmed on a large scale as well as operated several agricultural related businesses which failed at the same time, he decided to go back to school and get a degree in law. While sitting in his beautiful office I couldn't imagine this man could have ever had any self doubt. After all he was an attorney. After my question he leaned across his desk and looked puzzled.

"Why Barry for years I have respected you and never once thought you had I.S.I."

Shocked I realized that while I was looking down on myself others were actually looking up to me.

"My life," he continued, "was such a failure that I even had trouble deciding what clothes to wear. I literally had to start flipping a coin on all small decisions because indecision was too big of an obstacle for me to handle. But I really feel that everybody has I.S.I. unless they are incredibly successful. I believe that we are all too hard on ourselves, we need to get out from under the basket of guilt."

"What a remarkable thought," I said, "please go on!"

"Well for example, how many times do we feel guilty when we lie down for a nap? Why? How many of us feel guilty when we spend money on ourselves, regardless how small the purchase? My wife spends all her time with our two kids and taking care of our home, yet she is overcome with guilt every time she has to leave them. You see Barry, we create a lot of our own faults, most people are much better than they actually see themselves. We must stop focusing on our shortcomings and start concentrating on all the virtues that each and everyone of us possesses. After all inferiority blocks the flow of energy we need to become more successful."

"But how do we get out from under the basket, especially when it seems to have two tons on bricks on top of it?," I ask.

He leaned back and sorta grinned, "I don't have all the answers!"

"Do you think sometimes we actually find security in our inadequacy?" I ask.

Again he leaned on his desk, "It could be, if we feel inferior we often will not attempt the things that seem hard to us. One good rule of thumb to remember is that the good in us often outweighs the bad."

Next I talked to a former high school football coach turned super successful businessman, we were at a mutual friends house sitting by the pool when I sprang this question on him.

"Shoot Barry, I felt like such a hypocrite. I would go out day after day and tell those kids to be leaders, I begged them to excel, I taught the principle to be all you can be, yet I was a miserable failure. My marriage was on the rocks, I was dead broke, and worse of all I was ugly. I knew I could do better for myself and my family but I could come up with a dozen reasons why I couldn't. I found out a long time ago that there are three things that are real hard to do. 1. You will find it is awful hard to climb a fence leaning towards you. 2. It's hard to kiss a girl leaning away from you. 3. You can't help someone who doesn't want help."

"Wait a minute are you saying that we have I.S.I. because we want it?" I ask puzzled.

After spitting out his tobacco he gave me that look that all football coaches must have patented.

"I'm saying that a man will use any excuse available if what he's facing is uncomfortable. Self image is a great deceiver, it tells us we are not capable or not able of doing something that we are most always able to do. We must all learn to have a little more ego, we must become the masters of our destiny."

After compiling my notes I find that most everybody has I.S.I. but it can be improved or even abolished. I also realize that most people are much, much better that they believe and that regardless of what triggers I.S.I. if left unchallenged it will only grow worse, like a sore that won't heal. I pass this review on to you my sons in hopes that one day you will recognize your faults and your limits, but in knowing them you will work to improve them and not use them as an excuse not to succeed. The degree of your Inadequate Self Image is ultimately controlled by only you.

A GOOD, GOOD MAN

Have you boys ever been down in the dumps? Well you probably wouldn't be my sons if you didn't. It's not a very good trait to have but so many of my family suffers from it. I use to battle with depression, it was a daily ritual, I had to fight to keep a positive outlook on life. So many times I would find myself on an emotional roller coaster, one day I would be sky high, the next I would be lower than a snakes belly in a wagon rut. But let me remind you boys of this, if you can't control your emotions, then you are out of control.

It was an overcast Spring day, humid, it looked like rain. I was turning land at the Johnson place and boy was I down. Who knows what caused it that day, maybe it was finances, perhaps someone spoke a harsh word to me, it could have even been something that was going on in the church. Have you ever noticed that it's not the big major problems that get us down? Oh sure all of the above mentioned were real enough, but certainly not worth worrying over. Regardless of what triggered it, I was down and out and just wished life was better. All of a sudden my plow struck something beneath the earth! With a bellow of black smoke and a jerk of the tractor, the large flat rock came rolling out of the ground. It was a very unusual looking rock and I made a mental note to examine it on my next round.

I put the rock on the back of my plow, and took a rag and began to rub its smooth surface, suddenly I realized that it was a very old tombstone. I took out my knife and began to trace out the weather worn letters. It simply gave a man's name, that he had died in 1889, and then these words;

"He was a good, good man." I looked up and around at the fertile bottom land. Whose home had it once been? Had this man been a farmer also? Did he leave behind a grieving wife and child?

Had he lived through the terrible war that divided our nation? Had he lived through the poverty and humiliation that followed the rage of Sherman's army? Had he seen the Indians driven off this land? So many questions and no answers. What did I know about this man? That he was a good, good man. Not a better than average, not just a good man, but someone had thought enough of his life to have put he was a good, good man. What a fine epitaph. What will they say about you and me when our time is over here on this earth. Wouldn't it be wonderful if someone thought enough about me to engrave in stone that I had been a good, good man. I carefully carried the stone to a nearby clump of trees and gently laid it down. I had no way of knowing where the actual grave was but I wanted to leave the stone as closely as possible to the remains of this good, good man. Suddenly my day seemed a little brighter, a load seemed to have been lifted. This isn't a dress rehearsal, this thing we know as life is the real thing and we have no idea how long it will last. What we do with every day, every minute is important. What they put on our tombstone will reflect the type of life that we have lived.

As I go home this evening I will be met at the door by two healthy, happy boys who love their daddy. My wonderful wife will be cooking supper. Our home will be warm, safe, and familiar. How often I needlessly invite worries into my life, sometimes it seems as if I invite them in for entertainment. I hope you boys will dwell on the good things of life, after all they are the important things, everything else will fade with the passing of time.

That man whose grave marker I held in my hands probably never thought his life would have an impact on someone a hundred years later. But every time I start feeling blue I remember those words. I never knew the man, but I knew the type of life he lived. From this day forward I will live everyday as if it were my last.

Chapter 4
IN WHOM DO YOU BELIEVE?

At the age of eight in a small community church, only a couple of miles from where I live today, I accepted Christ into my life as my personal Lord and Savior. A few days later I was baptized in a lake and officially joined the Baptist church. There was no drastic change in my life, my mother and father had brought me up in the church and lived a Christian life in front of me everyday, however my beliefs have taken a few twist and turns here and there that I'm sure is all part of growing older.

At first I guess I was pretty liberal, I believed that as long as you went to church on Sunday morning and gave a few dollars that you could live as you wanted the rest of the week. Later I developed the attitude that as long as you were a white Southern Baptist you would surely make it to Heaven. For years I believed in straddling the fence on most issues. But through a long period of learning, studying the Bible, and associating with strong Christians, I have reached a point in my spiritual life that I am well pleased with. I now take a stand on issues dealing with morality, and realize that regardless of denomination all Christians are working towards the same goals.

Being in the rural South, we take our beliefs strongly and fiercely defend our right of religious freedom. I took a few things that have made an impact on me spiritually and put them in words, in hope that one day they will act as both inspiration and a source of comfort to you boys.

WHAT ABOUT TOMORROW?

As I look at you boys now in your childhood I realize you have no worries and very little thought of tomorrow. How wonderful it is that you boys can feel so secure and happy in your world, unfortunately as you grow into adulthood you will find yourself wondering about more and more things that seem to complicate life.

A. J. Cronin once wrote, "Worry never robs tomorrow of its sorrow; it only saps today of its strength." I wish I had taken that statement to heart years before I did. Looking back I must have enjoyed worrying because I did it all the time. I worried about all the crops and all the livestock. I would stay awake worrying over money problems. I even worried about what was happening in soap operas. Soon it became habit and even though statistics prove that only 2% of what people worry about ever occurs, I was consumed with worry to the point that I made life miserable.

Christmas 1983 gave me plenty to worry about. My farm was failing horribly after three consecutive years of drought. Tom was a very sick baby, he had picked up a staff infection from the hospital. We were so broke that we couldn't pay attention and Carolyn's dad, Chirl, was deathly ill with cancer. It was during this time that my belief began to waiver, did God really care about me? Was life ever going to be any better? Your mother and I had put Christmas on hold that year. There was no tree, no gifts, no lights, no cards, no Christmas music, as far as I was concerned there was no need to celebrate the birth of Christ this year, after all, what did I have to be thankful for? Christmas was off.

Even though I didn't know that this would be Chirl's last Christmas with us, I knew my father-in-law was very sick. He had to go into Atlanta to have Oncology treatments every other day and it usually fell my lot to carry him. I really didn't mind, it gave me more time with my old friend, but still it was depressing me frightfully. I had come to know all of the nurses at the hospital well and all greeted us with Christmas cheer as we entered that Christmas eve morning. The weather outside was bitterly cold and I welcomed the opportunity to sit quietly in the warm waiting room and read. Suddenly a young lady came in and sat down in a chair next to me, as I looked around the waiting room I found it empty with the exception of two ladies that were there regularly. Why does she have to sit so close, I thought to myself. To my dismay she began to talk immediately, and what made it so bad was that she was happy! Couldn't she see that I wanted to be left alone? I was depressed and I wanted to enjoy it by myself.

She told me that her name was Helga, and that she had cancer. She began to ramble about her love for travel and flowers, she was talking ninety miles a minute and wanted me to engage in conversation badly.

"Have you bought all your presents yet?" she inquired.

"No," was my only reply.

"My goodness in only a few hours we will be celebrating the birth of our Saviour. I have to do all of my shopping early because I never know if I will be well enough later. Did I tell you that I have had cancer since I was thirteen? Oh yes I have had many stays in the hospital and unfortunately I can't get very far away because of my treatments. Don't you just love this time of year? Everyone seems so happy!

That did it! She had no right to invade my miserable state of being. She had no right to be so happy! I looked at her for the first time. She was a beautiful girl in her late teens or early twenties. She wore denim jeans which hugged her slim figure like a glove, a flannel shirt and a denim jacket. Her face was flawless, not a blemish on her fair complexion. She had deep blue eyes that sparkled and a cute turned up nose. She wore a red bandanna and it was clear to see that she had no hair, obviously loss from cancer treatments. I then made a statement that I regretted the moment that I spoke it, "Helga, how can you be so happy? This could be your last Christmas!"

As we starred eye to eye a radiant smile broke across her face, "Why Barry, how do you know that this won't be your last Christmas?"

What had she said to me? It hit me like a ton of bricks. Was I promised another Christmas? Of course not, yet I had never thought of that. Tomorrow may not come. Chirl might outlive me. This was a new realization, I needed to think.

The head nurse, Mrs. Conner came to the door, "Helga, time to go."

Helga stood and gently touched my hand, "The greatest gifts we possess are found within. Barry, God loves you, and so do I." She turned and walked away.

She was right! Why worry about all the things to come? Worry and faith are the same thing, they just move in opposite directions – worry toward satan, faith toward God. My life changed instantly, suddenly I was excited about life, today, this moment. But still it troubled me how she knew my name, I hadn't told her, oh well Christmas was back on! I couldn't wait to get back home and tell your mother.

After telling Carolyn all about my experience she was thrilled. She suggested that we buy Helga a gift and give it to her on our next visit to the hospital. What a wonderful life we so often take for granted. Only we possess the ability to control our emotions. I made a promise to myself, from this moment forward I will not waste another minute worrying about things that may or may not happen, from now on I will concentrate on today and with Gods help make all of them good. That Christmas was a great one! Tom was getting better, we still had Chirl, I still had my beloved farm, but best of all I now had a new outlook on life.

The day after Christmas your grandfather and I went back to the hospital with a special present for a special girl. I had no idea if I would see her or not, after all I had never seen her before, however I was sure that one of the nurses would be glad to see that she received it. After a quick search around for her I stopped at the nurses desk to inquire. I couldn't believe that none of the nurses knew who I was talking about! Although I only knew her first name I described her perfectly. Then I saw Mrs. Conner coming down the hall, quickly I ran to her, I began to ask her about Helga. She looked at me strangely.

"I have never had a patient of that description. I don't even know any Helga's. Excuse me, I must be about my work."

I was stunned. Was I crazy? Had I been under so much pressure that I was imagining things? I stumbled to the waiting room and sat down, God what is happening to me? Just then I remembered the two ladies that had been in the waiting room on Christmas Eve, I approached them and ask them if they remembered seeing me with the young lady, "Why yes, we were wondering who she might be, we had never seen her before," they replied. Returning to my seat I noticed a Bible placed by the Gideons laid open on the table beside me, as I looked down the words from Acts 12:15 leaped out at me "...It is his angel."

I honestly believe to this day that I encountered an angel that Christmas Eve, and she had delivered a message that has made me a better man. I have come to realize that

Gods interest in us is much more steadfast and trustworthy than our interest in Him. How much are you willing to let God do for you? I will ask you boys to live life carefully, because you never know when you might entertain angels.

THE WRECK

Our lives are but dying embers, here for a while and then gone. When we are gone only memories will remain. Every life is filled with turning points, meeting your mother was a turning point in my life, my decision to follow Christ was a turning point, the birth of you boys was a turning point. But every now and then events will happen that will shape our lives, and yes maybe even shape our faith. So it was on that Spring day in 1988.

I had just finished a great lunch with you and your mother at our home and decided to go into town that afternoon. While driving along I felt great that day, things were going good and many of my problems seemed behind me. It seems so often that our lives are made up of storms. A storm however might be a good sign, you know you are not conquered as long as you are in a storm. Many of our storms are just opposition to the miracles that are fixing to occur in our lives. As I topped the hill I saw that an accident had just happened. The small car had just came to a stop on its top in a neighbors wheat field. Dust still clouding the sky and wheels still spinning on the overturned car, I jumped from my truck to see if I could help. Obviously the car had been traveling much too fast and the driver had lost control.

The first person I saw was a man who had been ejected from the car, he seemed all right other than a possible broken leg, he begged me to help his brother and nephew still trapped in the car. The smell of gasoline was strong and I feared a fire. The child begin to cry as I got on my knees to look in, the young boy, five or six years old, appeared to be badly hurt as I pulled him from the wreckage. Others began to stop and I felt a great sense of relief, its always good to have help in times of tragedy. I was assured that an ambulance had been called as I began to crawl back into the car for the father of the boy.

The car must have rolled several times, because the roof was smashed close to the body. It was very cramped and all I could do to wedge myself in. At least I was not afraid of a fire now that others with fire extinguisher stood nearby. I moved slowly on my belly over the broken glass, dirt, and transmission fluid until I reached the man lying on his back. A quick survey of the situation made me sick, his left arm was pinned beneath the hood and the ground, his legs were hopelessly lodged, every time his heart beat a stream of blood gushed from a slash on his throat. He was alive and conscience but couldn't make a sound. I removed my shirt and put around his neck, I started to back out, I needed air, when he grabbed my arm with his free hand. He didn't want me to leave and I knew that I had to stay. The words of Andrew Jackson ran through my mind, "One man with courage makes a majority." He needed me to be strong and I needed him to be strong. We looked each other in the eye. I heard the boy crying, I knew the father did to as tears ran down the side of his face.

"Hang on friend, help is on the way," I said.

As he starred at me I knew and he knew he was dying. I heard the sirens come to a halt as the paramedics rushed to the side of the child. I turned my head to watch them work. They were so efficient, such achievers. It dawned on me that none of us are born achievers, achievers have to be made. The men weren't born with the knowledge to achieve the task at hand, they had to learn it, just as you and I have to learn to achieve any of our goals. The greatest force on earth is the human soul set on fire to help another human being.

I looked back at the man, I did only what I knew to do, I prayed aloud.

"Oh Lord, I don't know this man or his condition. I don't know if he knows you in the free pardon of sin. If not I pray that he ask forgiveness of his sins and shortcomings.

If he is one of your children I pray that you prepare to receive him into your kingdom and grant unto him all the treasures you have in store for him. Amen."

He squeezed my arm so hard that it hurt, and then the tears stopped, a beautiful smile came to his face, he released his grip and pointed with one finger skyward. And then in the glass, the dirt, the blood, and the oil, he died. His arm fell to the ground, his eyes closed and the blood stopped flowing. I crawled out of the wreckage and looked at my watch, only fifteen minutes had past since I first saw the accident. How quickly can our lives be changed. I walked over to the other man being loaded into the ambulance.

"Was your brother a Christian?" I ask.

"Not that I know of." Was his reply.

I smiled and put my hand on his shoulder, "I believe he is now." I said as I turned and walked back to my truck.

What a strange feeling I was having, not one of sorrow or grief, but a sense of comfort, of knowing that some how, some way, God had used me in a very special way. I had been at the right place at the right time, to help someone reach a decision as to where eternity would be spent.

I had seen death before and have seen it since, but never have I felt what I was feeling then. You see God gives us all many chances. The One who created you and me doesn't have the words looser, hopeless, incurable, no chance, or beyond repair in His vocabulary. He gives us all the choice, it is up to us to decide. What lies ahead or behind is not nearly as important as what lies within.

AT THE TOP OF THE STAIRS

Matt, last night you taught me a lesson I shall never forget. I had just finished my shower and stepped out of the second floor bath to find you waiting patiently for your dad to appear. There you sat, already in your PJs wanting your daddy to come downstairs and hold you till you could fall asleep. Your blue eyes were so heavy with sleep that they showed no excitement as I walked past you.

"Come on sport," I casually called over my shoulder as I headed for the stairway.

You are only two years old, about three foot tall, and less that forty pounds, but I was about to learn an important lesson in faith from you. You see we can learn from anybody if we are willing to.

As we approached the top of the stairs we stood side by side looking down the flight. The house in which we live is known as Gilreath Manor, a huge rambling turn of the century farm house. Seven steps descend to the landing, turn, and thirteen more brings you to the downstairs hallway. As we stood there you lifted up your left hand waiting for me to respond. You didn't need my hand, you had been going up and down these steps all your life, but by taking your fathers hand you find the courage to run, jump, skip, or take bold steps on your journey down. After I hesitated for a few seconds you looked up with those 'puppy dog' eyes to make sure I was still there. Not being able to resist another moment I reached down and grasp your outreached hand firmly. As we went down together I could not help but think how we as adults depend on our heavenly Father's hand everyday.

You knew beyond a shadow of a doubt that I would take your hand, but even as you looked up you were expressing your desire for my help. Don't I depend on God for everything that I do? When the crops need rain, don't I know He is waiting there to respond? When I am lonely and needing to be comforted, will He not reach down to me? How about the other day when I was having problems making heads or tails out of that budget, did he not grasp my hand boldly and give me direction? Sure we depend on him, many times take Him for granted, when we reach up. Just as you faced a problem of descending the stairs as a short legged two year old, you will face other problems in life where your earthly daddy can not help. Just remember all you have to do is reach up, take His hand, and do it anyway. Let me share with you a few lines that were written by an unknown author.

DO IT ANYWAY

If you do good, you will be accused of selfish motives.
    Do good anyway.
Success will win you false friends and true enemies.
    Succeed anyway.
The good you do today will be forgotten tomorrow.
    Do good anyway.
Honesty and frankness cause you to be vulnerable.
    Be honest and frank anyway.
The biggest people with the biggest ideas can be shot down by the smallest people with the smallest ideas.
    Think big anyway.

People favor underdogs but follow top dogs.
Fight for some underdog anyway.
What you spend years building may be destroyed overnight.
Build anyway.
People need help but may attack you if you try.
Help them anyway.
Giving the world the best you have may get you kicked in the teeth.
Give the world your best anyway.

I arose last night and went to the bed where you boys were asleep. Finding you safe I wandered through the dark old house to the glass front door. Looking out, the Winter night was alive with sparkling stars, a brilliant moon, and a bitter cold wind that was swirling leaves in the front yard. Only a few days remained until Christmas, such a happy time of year. My mind began to race, will we ever get those beans out of the field across the street? Will there be enough money for gifts this year? Will I be able to keep this drafty old house warm enough for Carolyn and the kids?

And then my thoughts turned back to little Matt at the top of the stairs and his faith. There in the darkness I stretched my hands skyward knowing my heavenly Father was waiting to grab them firmly, and lead me down the unknown stairway of my life.

DADDY

Letters to you boys wouldn't be complete without mention of a very special man in our lives, my dad. You boys have already become very close to your "paw-paw," but the man that I call daddy has done so much for me, our family, the community, Christianity, and our county that it would fill volumes, however I would like to list a few of the things he has taught me over the years. I believe God allows us all the decision to love, through love my dad has, and still is, teaching me many invaluable lessons.

I think the greatest lesson a dad can give is that of a life lived for Jesus. Day in and day out my dad demonstrated what a Christian life should be. Through good times and bad, sickness and health, tragedy and financial hardship, I've seen him hold firm to his solid rock like faith. The greatest witness any of us could have is that day to day walk that many boast of but few possess. Much as an umpire will hold to his conviction of an unpopular call, my dad will not sway in his decision to live a Godly life.

He taught me how important it is not to give up. How ever tough the going gets one must never throw up his hands in despair. I love the speech once made by the great statesman Winston Churchill when he declared, "Never, never, quit." Often I've watched him tear down a piece of equipment, not knowing the problem, but with a bulldog type attitude that he would fix it, regardless of how hard the task.

He taught me how important it is to continue to learn. Even though he never had a desire for more college credits or other degrees, he always wanted to learn more. His deep studies into the Bible has rewarded him with a reputation of being somewhat of an expert. His knowledge of Theology and doctrines have impressed more than one preacher. Not only did he study the writings of the Holy scriptures, he would always keep books around on electronics, radio and TV repair, and anything else he thought might come in useful. This behavior instilled within me an appetite for knowledge. Only God can give wisdom (of which he gave my dad a double portion) but we can vastly improve our lives by being involved in the continuing of our education.

He taught me about work, even though it is a four letter word it isn't dirty. He has always believed that the harder you world the luckier you get. One of the things we must do is to pursue a career that is interesting to us and is compatible with our abilities and our talents. We must make ourselves do things that other people won't do. The biggest difference between a winner and a looser is that the winner did some things that were uncomfortable. I love the old saying, "Never try to teach a pig to sing. It waste your time and annoys the pig!"

He taught me not to be afraid to ask for help. One of the greatest problems faced by youths and adults is that they let pride keep them from accomplishing their goals. Often I've watched dad struggle trying to find an answer to a particular problem. When at last he resolved that he could not find a solution he would not be embarrassed to ask someone who might know. The Bible teaches us to seek wise counsel, if we would do this more often we could benefit from the mistakes of others rather than having to make them ourselves.

He taught me that I should enjoy the journey as much as the destination. So often in life we make the road to success miserable and at times unbearable. Try to enjoy the journey along lifes way, it makes getting your reward all the more special. After all it is the climb, not reaching the top, in which we will develop.

He became my "Hero." How sad it is that many kids have to look for role models in sports figures and entertainers. My dad was so special to me when I was growing up that I wanted to be just like him. I wanted then, and still do today, to win his approval in all that I do. Many times when facing a tough situation in life I ask myself, "How would dad do this?" We must all develop the habit of associating with successful people. Find the people you admire the most and spend time with them, it will be of great value to your success. The Bible in Proverbs 15:22 speaks of how important others can be to us.

He taught me about the priorities in life. At an early age I discovered that real "men" were those who loved their family and their God while striving to make this world a better place for all. A person should never get the first three priorities out of order, they must remain, your God, your family, and then your business. All too often people try to switch them around only to find that it won't work any other way. When setting goals for your life make sure that they won't interfere with the priorities that keep your life in perfect balance.

He taught me how to be a leader. A leader is not a personality or a title, it is simply being willing to do what needs to be done without being told. I can't ever remember my dad asking me to do something he was not willing to do. If I ever felt unsure of how to do something he took his time and patiently showed me how so that I would always remember. That's what a leader really is. One thing he always stressed is to do more than is expected of you, this is guaranteed to make you a leader.

He taught me to put the past behind me. It's true you can learn from your mistakes but don't dwell on them unless that is the direction you want your life to go. He told me onetime that one of the hardest things to do in life is to quit trying to undo something that has already been done. If our God can forgive and forget our past mistakes we should certainly be willing to try.

And last but not least, he taught me to be myself. Oh sure there have been times when I have put on aires and tried to impress others but I could always close my eyes and see my dad. Be all you can be, but remember God created you to be you, there is not another person in this world exactly like you. God gave us the gift of life, what we make out of it will be our gift to God.

My dad is a strong man with a tender heart. I've seen the same rough hands do hard manual labor and minutes later caress a small kitten. He is a man who loves life but is ready to go when God finishes his mansion. I never really knew how much that I loved my dad until you boys came into my life. It is my prayer that you fellows can grow up to be much the same man as my daddy.

THE POWER PRAYER

One of my favorite subjects to read about is prayer. Books and books have been written about this phenomena and I enjoy reading other peoples view on this great power that all Christians possess. I firmly believe that prayer is the most powerful source that a human can use. I've seen prayer answered many times. I've seen miraculous healings that I attribute directly to prayer. I've had answers to difficult questions come moments after I had prayed. Time after time we've had friends and loved ones come to know the loving, saving, grace of Jesus after many prayers had been made in their behalf.

I can still see in my minds eye, when you Tom, as a small child, would come and kneel next to me as I prayed daily. You might not have known exactly what I was doing, but you knew it was very important. I am grateful every time we sit down to a meal that you boys insist upon giving grace before we eat.

A person can pray anytime, anywhere, and in any position. I find that my favorite time for prayer is first thing in the morning. I love to sit down at my desk and read from Gods word, then to embrace God in conversation. Every so often I experience what I like to call the power prayer.

I realize that God hears us whenever, wherever we pray, but so many times I go to the Lord in prayer and regardless of how hard I try, I find it hard to find the closeness of God. And then there are those sweet precious occasions when, from the moment I fall on my knees, that I can feel the presence of God. I can feel Him drawing me closer and closer until I feel warm, comfortable, and strong. It is during these times that I pour my heart out to Him. I tell Him of my problems and ask for solutions. I ask for wisdom and strength. During these fantastic conversations I feel God's reassurance that He is in control of my life. Some of my best ideas have come immediately following a power prayer. After one of these special prayers I feel a mixture of excitement, power, and exhaustion.

I love these times spent with my heavenly Father. We must realize that we are more than just blood and bone, we are full of hopes and dreams. The greatest obstacles in our lives can be overcome with valuable time spent on our knees. I love the motto used by the auxiliary of The Gideons International, "We will stay on our knees to keep the Gideons on their feet." I think this would be a great motto for all of us to adopt for our business and personal lives.

Chapter 5
WHAT HAPPENED?

Have you ever noticed how our lives are affected by events? Maybe it was a wondrously planned gala, or a sudden tragic shock. It might have happened when you least suspected it or maybe it was something you had been praying about. Whatever the setting, often our lives will be touched or even changed, by an event we can so easily recall.

Have you ever found yourself knee deep in a mess of blues and wondered if life was worth living? Have you ever stopped and wondered if your goals and dreams are really worth the price you are having to pay? Of course you have. But then something happened that made you say, "YES IT IS!"

These times in our lives can prove to be very beneficial or very detrimental depending on how you handle them. One thing we must do is to take these opportunities as a time to learn. There are two different ways to learn. First you can learn by experience, things that have actually happened to you. Second you can learn by wisdom, that is you learn from the events in other peoples lives. Which brings us to the point that many of these events will be with other people or even brought about by others. Even though you boys have heard me say this before, it bears repeating – strive to surround yourselves with good people. Always be a student of the one that has succeeded before you. The Bible stresses over and over how important this is. In

Proverbs 13:20 we are told how to be wise, in Proverbs 11:4 we are told how to be safe. I love the saying by Paul Harvey, "If you want big fleas hang out with big dogs!" We will never know how much we can effect others by an encouraging word. We can actually be a part of someone's miracle and not even know it.

So let me take a few pages to tell you about some of the events that stand out in the mind of your dad. Many of them came when I was least expecting them. Sometimes I kept mementos of the events, other times I just committed them to memory. One thing is for sure, we never know how the events of tomorrow will alter our lives.

THE BATTLE

From 1980 til 1982 your mother and I crisscrossed the state campaigning for one of our friends to be elected the next governor. During that time I found myself consumed with the issues of the day. Politics had always fascinated me and now they had become part of my daily life. In the Spring of 1982 while dinning with my parents, I surprised everyone with my intentions to run for the House of Representatives of our state. Although no one seemed thrilled with my decision, mom, dad, and Carolyn all agreed to give me 100% of their support in my quest for a seat in the State Capitol.

On a beautiful June day we traveled to Atlanta to officially announce my intentions. It was on this day as I walked those hallowed halls of the great building that I began to question my decision. Did I actually believe that I could beat out two distinguished attorneys and one successful business man for that position? Why, I was no more than a dirt farmer with a dream. It was also on that day that my critics began to predict my chances as slim to none. One so called friend guessed that I would come in dead last.

The summer loomed ahead as a huge obstacle course of handshakes, bar-b-q's, and speeches. The weather was hot and dry that summer as I spent hours canvassing our county. There were signs to put up and people to meet. There were babies to kiss and promises to make. My parents worked non stop telling others about their son. My wife would walk miles knocking on doors and hours on the radio telling the public how much she loved and respected her husband. Carey, our hired hand, not only did my part of the farm work, but spent all of his free time handing out cards and asking for votes. And then their was Theresa who went from farm secretary to campaign secretary overnight. She would prepare my meals and lay out my clothes. She kept the schedule and made sure that I was where I was supposed to be. And when I became overwhelmed with the pressures of the battle she would sit and patiently reassure me that I was the best candidate. I was ill prepared for the many speeches I would have to give and the debates I would have to fight. I stuck to my beliefs on the hard issues and let people know where I stood on the moral issues of drunk driving, gambling, and abortion. The days and weeks drug by til election day came in August. A small crowd gathered at our home to listen to the election returns from a local radio station. When it was over I had come in second, I was in a runoff with one of the attorneys!

The next three weeks were the worst of my life. The campaigning was vicious, I had shocked a great many people by getting this far. As they planned their strategy my troops rallied, and now I had a whole army of wonderful caring people out working in my behalf. During this time I began to find out who my friends were. A friend of many years who had been like a brother, campaigned for my opponent and spread cruel lies about me. Anonymous phone calls would bring forth insults to my wife and mother. Local officials offered me bribes if I would only step aside. I remember one day going down to the spring, sitting on the ground and weeping. Why was I doing this? Was I now hurting the family which loved me? Theresa sought me out and gently put her arms around me, there was nothing to say. Only the man in the arena knows the feeling that comes during this time. The night before the election I went to the church, knelt at the alter and prayed. I did not pray for a victory, but rather for the results that would be the best for my family and myself. I thanked God, not for the position I was in, but for the opportunity to dream and to live in a country where those dreams can come true.

As a crowd of supporters gathered at a local farm supply store the results began to pour in. The first precinct reported me a winner by a big margin, then the next the same, and the next the same! Victory was staring me in the face, a hundred plus people cheered their support. I would not accept the victory until every ballot was counted. Going into the counting of the absentee ballots I was leading by a hair. But then the final results were in. Out of nearly ten thousand votes cast I had lost by one hundred and one votes. As I took the microphone I looked around at the stunned crowd, a few crying, no one speaking. My heart hurt, tears stung my eyes, I had let a lot of good people down. Theresa and my sister wept, mother and dad held one another, Carey hung his head in disbelief, my wife stood proud and strong. I then gave my speech conceding the election to my opponent. For the first time in my life I had lost, I didn't like the feeling. Could I have done more? We shall never really know.

Your mother collapsed into bed that night exhausted. I couldn't sleep. I got up and walked through the house, I felt so alone, so ashamed of my failure. I walked out onto the porch and looked across the moon lit fields and suddenly I remembered the prayer I had prayed the night before. God had answered in the only way He could, with my defeat. Now I was feeling better, this was Gods will, He knew best. I sank to my knees and began to pray, "Oh Lord, I thank you for the blessings you have bestowed upon me. Thank you for the opportunity to display my political right. Thank you for allowing me to live in a country where the people can elect the person of their choice. And Lord give to the victor a generous outpouring of your blessings. Amen."

THE SENATOR AND I

It has been a great privilege and honor of mine to have been acquainted with several great men of political distinction. Over the years your mom and I have laughed with governors, dined with agricultural commissioners, and once when you were but a small boy Tom, we had a congressman and his family spend the day with us on our farm. How splendid it is to call these men who help run our country your friend. I have found out from the association that these special men are just like you and me. They have needs and wants just like us. The pressure they are under sometimes seems inhumane for any man to have to bear. Often I have found that they want and desire just to have someone that they can fellowship with without having to talk shop or make promises. I remember one time when congressman Darden, from the seventh political district of Georgia, fell asleep on our couch with your grand dad and myself in the room! Upon awakening from his peaceful sleep he was quiet embarrassed. We assured him that we felt only joy that he could feel so comfortable in our company.

During my young adult years I became very close to United States senator Herman Talmadge from Georgia. We conferred often by phone and letter What a thrill it was to associate with this great statesman. He had been involved in politics all of his life following in the footsteps of his famous father Eugene Talmadge, former governor of our great state. While in Washington D.C. on business I took the opportunity to stop by his office for a visit. Being informed by his secretary that the senator was still in a congressional hearing, I decided to wait there in the office for his return. This was a very troubled time for my friend as he was undergoing a grueling investigation by a congressional committee. It has often been my opinion that we waste far too much time and money in this country trying to humiliate our leaders instead of giving them the support they need. I took this time to look around the finely appointed office and soon found myself relaxed on the soft leather sofa. In a few minutes the office door swung open as the senator entered and removed his coat. Immediately he came over to where I stood with an outstretched hand.

"So good to see you my friend. Please tell me how you and your family are doing. How's your mother and father?" The words rolled smoothly out of his mouth with his warm Southern drawl.

I couldn't help noticing how tired and old he looked. And with all the agony he was going through, he was still genuinely concerned about my welfare. It is the trait of all leaders to be more interested in others than themselves. After he seated himself behind his huge wooden desk he lit one of his famous cigars and questioned me about all of his friends back in Bartow county. We talked about farming for a few minutes then he ask what he could do for me. I replied that it was the other way around this time, what could I do for him? The hour was late so I ask him if I could take him to dinner, which he refused politely then he seemed to relax back into his chair as if suddenly he was exhausted. After several minutes of silence the once great orator began to speak.

"Barry there are only three things in this world comparable to politics. Hand to a hand combat, killing rattlesnakes, and fighting forest fires."

"You're a mighty brave man senator."

He made a tent with his fingers and smiled.

"A truly brave man, Barry, must also possess a lot of fear. Brave men are not fearless, that is one of the keys to success."

"Are you afraid senator?" I asked.

"Yes I am Barry. I'm afraid that all that I have strived to do in my life will be forgotten and I will only be remembered for my mistakes. I have never been overjoyed in my victories and I've never let depression defeat me, I've just tried to do my duty for my country."

Here before me was a man facing great adversity and yet he still wanted to serve others. His enemies felt as if they had the upper hand, but some how I suspected different. He had been called a born leader, he was nothing of the kind, he was just a man with fixed methods and a strong will. I remember the scripture in Romans 12:15 that says to "weep with those that weep." I certainly wanted to, but also knew that it wouldn't help.

"You have a lot of good folks back home that love and respect you." I said. "We're all rooting for the senator that we elected."

"Maybe that man doesn't exist anymore." was his immediate response. Then he leaned forward." In every race some one must win and some one must lose, but all must run. My course is not yet completed and I refuse to quit before it is done!"

The phone rang and soon he was asking another constituent about his health and the welfare of his mother and father. I excused myself and walked out of his office for the last time, he was later defeated for re-election.

The senator, at the time of this letter, is still doing quiet well living on his middle Georgia farm. I think often of that day and of our conversation in the capitol city.

That event has given me courage when the going got tough. I had seen a man face adversity and not back down. I have learned that it is okay to be afraid because that is part of being brave. I also now realize that regardless if we are behind in the game of life we must stride on because it is too soon to quit!

THE JOURNEY

Tom's great journey started this morning. His first official day of school. I stood on the front porch, bathed in the bright morning sun, as your mother prepared to drive you to school. Our emotions on this day are so different. You Tom, are full of excitement and anticipation while I am scared. I choke back tears as the car pulls from the farm knowing that your days of innocence are coming to an end. Where did the time go? Only yesterday we brought you home from the hospital wrapped in a blue blanket. Have I spent my time with you wisely? Or did I waste it on unimportant "business"?

To you this is the beginning of a new adventure. If you only knew how many hours you will spend in the classrooms, I dare say we could drag you to school. Many years, twelve, sixteen, or more lie in front of you as a great challenge. You will be forced to learn things that you will never possibly need to know. I remember how important they made the SAT test sound in high school. This test they said, would ultimately decide my future. When I borrowed my first $100,000 the banker could care less about my SAT scores. Once in college I was made to memorize some of the writings of Shakespeare, I have never been ask in any business dealings to repeat it. So much you learn from books and blackboards is useless. Son if they were to teach you about success principles and how to survive in the real world many of your heartaches would never occur.

I worry about all those teachers who will have an affect on your life. The power they possess over tender minds is unbelievable. I had many great teachers, but I also had a few that only cared about making a student feel lower that a well diggers shoes. I had a high school counselor to actually tell me that I would never amount to much! She told me that I couldn't farm, and that her professional opinion was that I would have to spend my life as a laborer. I am so thankful that I was not gullible enough to swallow her venom.

She was wrong! But I've often wondered how many young lives she could have destroyed.

Then there are those other children. Unfortunately you will get most of your education from them. I pray that you will be strong enough to refuse to do some of the things your comrades will beg you to try. I hope you will know what to do when others laugh at you and poke fun. I encourage you not to follow the crowd, be brave enough to stand out on your own convictions and merits.

As the dust settles in the drive I pause to think back upon the great leaders of the past. How many of them had relied on public education to make them the hero's they became? I realize that you will always look to your daddy as the man who knows all. And I realize that I am a man that knows very little about being a good daddy. I will make it my pledge from this day forward to always try to be the man that you think I am. I will try to be more sufficient as the days go by. I must learn how to be a living example of how a man should act.

Yes son, a new chapter in your life started today, but a new one started for me too. The sudden realization that being a father is more than providing for your needs, it's earning your trust and respect. I'm sure that you will turn out to be a great student, but I can only wonder what kind of dad I will be. Only time will reveal.

THE BREAKING POINT

At a dinner meeting the other night the discussion at the table somehow turned to suicide. My colleagues were all of the same opinion, that it could never happen to them. One even remarked that he had no use for anyone who could ever attempt such a dastardly deed. I could only smile and remember what had happened to a young man that I once knew. As they talked my mind drifted back to the time when this particular fellow realized that everyone has a breaking point. Everyone may not reach that point, but everyone has one. This young man had all the seemings of wealth, he had a nice car, a nice house and a nice dog. He had quickly rose to the top of his profession, twice being named the best at what he did. He had been nominated for "Young Man of the Year," in his community, where he was greatly loved. Banks begged for his business, magazines and newspapers eagerly published his writings. His friends numbered into the hundreds, he and his wife were invited to all the right gatherings. Then suddenly the winds of fortune changed. The economy tightened and his business interest begin to suffer. He borrowed more and more money just trying to survive, but to no avail. The dark clouds of depression began to settle in as he watched his world crumble. The death of a loved one is painful, but to a person who owns a dying business the pain is just as real and just as bad.

He searched for months for a solution to his problems only to find none. He got further and further behind in debts and now the bankers no longer sought his business. The invitations to prominent dinners ceased and many of his so called friends now only had pity on him. He was overcome with grief and went for months with no sleep, he only ate occasionally, and the headaches got worse and worse. His wife went to work at a job that she hated just so they could buy food and diapers for their new born baby. He found himself confined to the house taking care of a sick baby most of the time. Quite a change for a man who had been use to working 90 to 100 hours per week at four different business operations.

The waitress poured me another cup of coffee. The conversation around me had changed, but as I sipped the steaming contents of the cup I found myself still thinking of that tragic time in the young man's life.

As the months drug by he lost more and more of his assets. Two attorneys begged him to file bankruptcy, but pride and a desire to do what was right was forcing him to liquidate all of his belongings. One early spring morning he took his sick baby to the doctor, the weight of the whole world seemed to be on his shoulders. He took the prescription from the doctor realizing that he couldn't afford the medicine. On the way home he decided to stop by and see a business acquaintance whom he considered a friend. His friend was like Job's friends and only found fault with the young man. The young man returned to the home which he was living in, it had already been sold, the people who bought it were nice enough to let him stay there until he could find a place to go. The baby was crying and burning up with a fever. Gently he laid his son on the bed as he hurried to answer the phone. On the other end he found a bill collector bitter and angry. Suddenly a knock at the door. A sheriff's deputy handed him a law suit filed against him for failure to pay a particular bill. The baby cried and cried, what could he do? Where could he find the money for medicine?

He began to look around the house for something that he could pawn. But all had been sold, no TV, no microwave, no VCR, everything gone. Suddenly he remembered the gun in the nightstand, that's it, he could sell the gun. As he pulled the drawer open, there he found a 44 magnum, picking it up he opened the cylinder to find it loaded. Then a new thought entered his head, he was more afraid to live than he was to die. He had just ran upon his breaking point. He placed the barrel next to his right temple, pulled the hammer back...then he heard a voice as audible as he had ever heard, "Don't you quit! If you quit, who will raise the boy?"

He dropped to his knees and ask God for forgiveness. Then he wept and pleaded with God, "Oh God you have to do something, I can live without a house, I can live without a car, but God I can't live without hope! Man was never intended to live without hope!"

Then I reached down and picked you up Tom. I held you to my tear stained shirt and promised you that from that day forth you would never go hungry again, that you would never have to do without medicine again, a promise that I am still keeping today.

SAM

Our early married years on the farm were marvelous. Your mother had been reared in the city and up until the Fall of 1979 she had worked as an executive secretary in Atlanta.

Having her home as a full time farm wife was thrilling to me. That Fall we purchased a herd of sows and a prize boar and went into the hog business. Carolyn considered this as her business and did an excellent job with the operation.

Early the next year your mother chaperoned a group of high school boys to an agricultural workshop in South Georgia. It was on this trip that she purchased Sam. She called me one night very excited to inform me that she had purchases the big quarter horse for only $750. Sharing her excitement I assured her that I would make the 300 mile trip that weekend to bring him home.

My first sight of Sam was eventful. He was big, well over 16 hands. He was red, and he had a nice gait. Sam was a gelding and very gentle. From the time I loaded him on the trailer for his journey north I knew he was more than just another horse. We had a few horses before but never one this nice. Your mother and I both enjoy riding and having a new horse was exciting.

As the years went by Sam and I became great friends. I used him a lot around the farm and enjoyed many long rides with him. However it was your mother that had a special relationship with Sam. He belonged to her and he loved her as much as she loved him. In my minds eye I can still see them galloping across the fields together, Sam in perfect stride and your mothers long hair blowing in the breeze. Sam was a good horse with little or no temperament.

After Carolyn found out that she was expecting you Tom, she stopped riding at the doctors advice. So one Spring day I decided to move Sam to another barn and pasture on the other side of the farm. There the grass was green and lush, and I knew that he would find perfect contentment in his new dwelling. After plowing all day I decided to go check on the old boy to see if he needed anything. Much to my horror I found him on the ground threshing and kicking, completely covered with barbed wire. Obviously he had gotten his leg through the fence and got scared, by the time I had found him he had tangled himself in ten feet of the razor sharp wire.

Carolyn, a hired hand, the vet, and myself, cut wire from the animal for over an hour. The vet said that his chances for survival were slim and that we needed to stay with him as much as possible throughout the night. After a late supper your mother and I went back to the barn to find Sam down and in bad shape. All of our efforts to get him up failed. Finally at about midnight Sam died. That is the only time I can remember seeing your mother cry over the loss of an animal. The farm life has a way of toughening you so that the passing of an animal has little effect on you. But this horse had become our friend and our companion, now he was gone.

"Don't be unhappy," I said, "Sam doesn't hurt anymore." She drew a long breath and wiped her face with here sleeve. She looked at the still horse and stroke his mane.

"He was a good horse." she said.

Sam will always be a part of your mothers life. The time she spent with him will always give her pleasant memories and the realization that he will always be a little alive in her heart.

Chapter 6
ISN'T LIFE SWEET?

I think it is sad that we so often take life, with all it's mysteries and wonders, for granted. My long time friend Dave told me the other day about the invasion of Normandy of which he took part. For hours he laid on the beach while hundreds of his comrades fell dead. He said all he could think of was the smell of home and the singing of birds.

A friend of mine who had moped over the loss of a girlfriend for months, was involved in a serious car accident. After waking up in the hospital alive he suddenly realized how short life could be and amazingly his love life seemed very unimportant.

As I sit here at my desk and write, you are busy Tom, working on a doghouse for your new puppy. I wonder what life would be like without you boys. There wouldn't be any Santa Clause or Peter Rabbit to prepare for. The house would be quiet and the upholstery would stay clean. There would be no questioning "why?" or "how?" and no snowmen to build. I thank God for you boys, you are a great part of our lives.

As we grow older we tend to notice more of the little things that make life such a pleasant experience. I took the time to write down some of my favorite memories.

REVIVAL

According to the Random House College Dictionary, Revival means a restoration, strength, an awakening of interest in religion. To me it brings back wonderful boyhood memories of the rural South and a small white church nestled in the edge of a pine forest. One of my favorite memories of my childhood stems from a revival meeting held in that sanctuary of God. I couldn't have been over six or seven years old and after an hour or so on those hard wooden benches I began to tire. I can still recall the fantastic feeling of scooting up real close to my daddy and him gladly welcoming me by putting his big right arm around me and pulling me near. I remember how close to him that I felt and how close God seemed. I can't recall if I did this every night, or just once, but I do remember thinking that surely God depended on my dad for a lot. Dad always sat up front and would frequently sound his approval with a hearty amen! I remember every time he would shout Amen, he would pat my shoulder and draw me a little closer. The amazing thing about this memory is that anytime now that I feel alone, or weak, or afraid, I think back to that ole time meeting and find myself finding lots of comfort there.

    As I reflect on my childhood I don't remember too much about the toys I received, or the clothes, but rather about family picnics where food and laughter was everywhere. About the time I was six years old and went hunting with daddy for the first time. Even though I was armed only with my new Daisy BB gun, I felt proud to be there with dad. I remember playing with your Aunt Bendy and being glad that she was my big sister. I remember drawing what I thought were pictures and having mama tape them to the refrigerator.

    I often remember mom and dad reading Bible stories to me at bedtime and wonder if that's were my love for the Bible and reading was formed. I remember mom and dad praying before every meal, I was grown before I realized that some people ate without blessing it first.

How blessed are the parents out there today that are forming the same memories for their children. Far too many times I have lost my patience with you boys when I should have taken time to explain things to you. I believe it was Thoreau who said that our lives are frittered away by detail. I'm sorry for all the times that I forgot you were but children and didn't understand the things that grownups do. I'm afraid too many times I've walked in a rush causing you boys to have to run on your short little legs to keep up, when in reality I had plenty of time to slow down and enjoy a lengthy stroll with my kids.

I think your uncle Wendell is a pretty good dad. Every time he goes camping he always takes your cousins with him because as he says, "They are my best friends." Even though he puts in long hours at the pharmacy he still finds time to build the boys a tree house and look at the stars at night. What do you reckon our world would be like if more daddies were like him?

I have found out that there are those people who think that life is a wonderful god given adventure to be enjoyed. These people seem to be full of energy and are generally always fun to be with. Then there are those who think of life as a chore. These people dread getting up in the morning and find it mighty easy to complain about almost everything. I can just about tell what kind of childhood each of these had. It's amazing what the love and companionship of parents can do for the life of a child.

I guess what I'm trying to say in all this is that I sure am proud of my "raisin" and of my parents. I hope I can give you boys the same memories you can go back and visit time and time again, they truly have a way of reviving you. And I pray that if one day God allows you the privilege of being fathers that you will live a life full and rewarding for your kids.

By the way Tom, you are six now, and often at church you will get tired and slide up close to me, I trust your memories will be as comforting as mine.

THE PRIVY

Way back when I was a senior in high school an event took place that has permanently lodged itself in my memory. Often I find myself thinking of that long ago day and it still forces me to smile.

One of my favorite teachers mother had passed away. Here in the south when someone dies we say that they passed away. Several of us boys decided that we should attend the funeral. I do not recall now whether we were so concerned for our teacher or if we just seized a convenient opportunity to miss an afternoon of school. It was a blustery March day. The sun was bright, but oh how the wind howled. Three of us boys had found a seat in the small rural Georgia church. The crowd had swollen to capacity as the first of three long tongued preachers started his oratory.

About ten minutes into the service Joe (the name has been changed to protect the innocent) leaned over to me and announced that he had to go to the restroom. Immediately I scolded Joe and told him to keep his seat. If he had left in the middle of the service it would have disrupted a perfectly good eulogy. In a few minutes ole Joe began to rook back and forth while holding his belly. He began to break out in a sweat and his skin took on an ashy grey color. His arms had goose bumps all over them and I knew that my friend was suffering. He just kept holding his belly with both arms, rocking back and forth and moaning in a low groveling voice. As the rest of the congregation marched pass the casket for viewing, Joe remained seated, all bent over and making muffled noises. Everyone but me thought that he was mourning and grieving. Even though I really felt for him I also knew that his leaving wouldn't show proper respect for the dead.

Just as the last preacher said amen, Joe jumped to his feet and raced for the door. On the porch he grabbed a small black boy by the overall calluses and gave him a hard shake.

In that day, folks of color were not allowed in this particular white church, so they had to stand on the porch to show their condolences. Joe demanded of the boy where the john was located. The young fellow, who seemed taken aback, pointed to the outhouse on the hill just above the cemetery. As Joe broke into a hard run to the toilet, he failed to hear the boy tell him not to forget to latch the door.

Well, just as the casket was being lowered into the grave, one of the preachers began to read the twenty-third Psalm. The crowd gathered in the cemetery was very quiet except for a few sniffles and sobs, when all of a sudden a hard March wind blew and BAM! BAM! BAM! The door to the outhouse which was only about twenty yards away, swung open! And there sat Joe. Of course being startled by the noise everyone, including the preacher stopped to stare. It wouldn't have been so bad but ole Joe just stood up in all his glory, reached out and closed the door!

It was nearly dark that night when we persuaded Joe to come on out of the privy. He wanted to make sure everyone, including the gravedigger, was gone. Needless to say this is still a touchy subject to Joe and to this day he refuses to discuss it.

You know boys I've often wondered how many lives would be changed today if we hadn't went to that funeral. I'm sure those that were there that day will never forget that memorial.

ENTREPRENEUR

A couple of years ago while on some business to rural South Georgia, I was introduced to a man as being a successful entrepreneur. I will never forget the slender built man with the bushy beard, peered out from under the grease stained Caterpillar cap, and with questioning eyes finally ask, "Is that anything like being a logger?"

Actually it is an awfully big word that means a person that organizes or manages a business or other enterprises. Over the years I have found myself engrossed in the business world. I can not think of anything else in the world that I had rather be than a successful businessman. Now boys don't ever let anyone ever tell you that a farmer is not a businessman. The American farmer is probably one of the sharpest business people you will ever meet, or else he won't be farming long.

I think one of our greatest pleasures in life should be our work. Nothing could be more frustrating than being stuck in a job that you hate. I have always been the type person who enjoys working and looks forward to the next venture. I will admit that there is something special about the men and women who refuse to settle for a life spent working for someone else. The desire for freedom beckons them to pursue ideas and opportunities that others would only scoff at. Yes sir, I believe that it is our God given privilege to work and provide for our families.

After coming out of a church service recently I had a young man to stop me and ask a question.

"Mr. Shinall aren't you involved in several different business ventures?"

After assuring him that I was he went on, "If you ever find a job where I could make some good money and not have to work, would you please let me know?"

My reply was that he had better try to get on welfare now, because that is the only way that I know of to get money for nothing. It makes me sick to see a young man of nineteen or twenty who wants something for nothing. This country was founded on hard work and effort, and that's the way it should be.

After several years of trial and error I would like to share with you boys five things I think you should look for in a business or career. Unfortunately I don't think many schools or colleges teach these, but I feel that the combination of the five will make your field of endeavor more enjoyable and profitable.

1. MONEY – If you were going to look for a job today, the first question you would ask is, how much does it pay? Money is important. If you are trading a portion of your life in order to make a living, make sure you make as much money as the market will bear. If you are starting a new business venture be sure and check out how much money the business could bring you. Run several budgets ranging from the best it could be, to the worst case senerio. Let me caution you on one thing. On giving birth to a business be sure to remember the law of Delayed Gratification. It might take a lot of work and effort before you start making a profit. As a farmer I understood this principle very well. When a farmer plants a seed he knows it will take several months before he makes a penny.

2. TAX BREAKS – I believe in paying taxes, my fair share that is. One of the best ways to make money is to

save it. If by having your own business you can create several tax advantages it is in your best interest. There are many businesses where you can legally deduct travel, entertainment, even clothing as a business expense. Whereas the common working man has no such luxuries.

3. SECURITY – Sadly many people hold onto their rut job by using the excuse of security. A man remarked to me recently that he had security because he had been employed at the same place for eleven years. Unfortunately what he had was a job unless he owned a portion of the company. If you have ever been hired, you can be fired! While working for a fortune 500 company I learned quickly that unless your last name was the same as the owners you could be replaced. We often think of professional people, such as doctors and lawyers, as being very secure in their profession. Actually if they don't see patients and clients, day in and day out, they have no way of earning a living. While visiting with a very successful surgeon the subject about security came up. I ask him how long he could live off his savings before he started having to sell things, his reply was about six months! I couldn't believe it. This very successful physician was as broke as I was! Only at a different level. But before you boys laugh, how much money do you have saved?

Set up a business that will have a residual income. That is, it will continue to make money whether or not you are there to run it or not.

4. DIVERSITY – This is one of the greatest laws of business. When I was twenty-five years old I knew none of my dreams were going to come true farming. Your mother and I were still living in a small house trailer, driving an old Chevrolet that had over one hundred thousand miles on it, and certainly not getting ahead. At that time I started to

diversify, getting involved in a trucking company, a livestock auction company, and a farm supply dealership. Life got better for a while, we got a house, a nice car, and a registered dog. We looked good, smelled good, and was broke! I found myself working ninety to one hundred hours per week and had no money to show for it. The key here is that diversity wasn't the key in itself, the business ventures I had started lacked all five ingredients, one without the other four won't help. The business or career that you choose must contain all five of the principles of a healthy business.

In searching for diversity, create added income without investing much money or time. Keep your mind open to new ideas. There are several multilevel marketing businesses that offer great diversity without much venture capital. I have found out that the best way to test a business is not only to check it out thoroughly but also spend time praying about it.

5. FREEDOM – Last but not least is your freedom. The best situation to be in is where you determine the amount of time that you want to work. All too often we let our business run us instead of us running it. Life is too short not to enjoy it.

I had a very successful business man tell me that if you were working six days a week in order to make a living, that you were in the wrong business. He said a smart man should be able to make a great living working only four days per week or less!

Sometimes we spend so much time making a living that we forget to make a life. Look for a venture that offers a flexible work schedule.

Life has so much to offer us if we only step out a little. I remember the classic film, *The Wizard of Oz*. Dorothy and her two friends were entering a forest which the yellow brick road lead thru. They began seeing things behind every tree and bush. They began to sing, "Lions, tigers, and bears, oh my! Lions, tigers, and bears, oh my!" It turned out to be no tigers or bears, and the lion was as harmless as a kitten. Isn't it amazing how we do the same thing in real life? After having an opportunity to better ourselves we waste a lot of time worrying about what could happen, or might happen, when in the end most of our lions are overgrown kitty cats. And if by some chance you do face a ferocious lion, our God is big enough to take care of him!

One of your greatest pleasures in life should be how we earn our living!

COUNTRY TREASURES

One of the great advantages of being a farmer is getting to work in the great outdoors, hand in hand with nature. A farmer's life is spent planting, harvesting, breeding, fixing, and relaxing in all four seasons. The beauty of the changing world combined with seasonal duties still excites me as much today as it did in my childhood. Let me share with you boys some of the things each season holds in store for me.

Spring on the farm is a time of rushing and long hours. This is the time of year that every farmer looks forward to as a new beginning. Seedbeds are prepared and the smell of freshly turned soil makes me hungry. The earth begins to change colors, pinks, bright greens, whites and yellows, decorate the landscape. The temperature is warm with the nights still chilly. It's a time when new born animals spring forth on wobbly legs and we marvel at life renewing each time. We begin to wear short sleeves and the kids want to go barefoot. April rains often slow planting schedules which gives us time needed for spring cleaning not only around home but in barns and shops. It's the season that gardens are being planted to provide food for our family all year. It means dressing up real special for Easter morning service and smelling steaks grilling on an open flame for the years first cookout. The first time grass is cut the smell of onions fill the air. With the finishing of planting a tremendous load seems to be lifted from the shoulders of the farmer.

As Summer rolls around life on the farm begins to take on a more relaxed atmosphere. Crops are up and growing and now comes the time of cultivation, weeding, and watching for insects. Soon around the first of July we "lay by" crops and begin getting up forage for the animals this winter. The nights are hot and the days are hotter. The world is now covered in a dark green veil. People begin setting on their porches until bedtime, often breaking beans, shelling peas, or peeling fruit. It's a time for fishing and eating, lots of eating.

The gardens provide a bountiful harvest of vegetables that find their way to the table daily this time of year. Watermelons are cut and folks often gather to churn homemade ice cream in a variety of flavors. The forth of July is always a big celebration and all of the farm hands stop this day to celebrate our independence with parades, bar-b-q's, and fireworks. One of the most pleasant things about the summer is the afternoon thundershowers that can pop up anytime, bringing with them moisture for the earth and cooling of temperatures. "Kattiedids" and "treefrogs" serenade us at night and the kids exhaust themselves chasing lighting bugs. We check the crops almost daily and begin getting excited about our upcoming harvest. As the summer draws to an end the days begin getting shorter.

Fall is my favorite time of the year. All of our efforts since spring come to an end. Nothing is more rewarding for a farmer than to harvest a good crop and see his hard efforts pay off. The days start before daylight and often last until the late night hours. It's going to the cotton gin or grain elevator and talking with many other farmers you only see once a year. Flannel shirts feel good and a fire at night takes the chill out of the house. The trees are an array of different colors and fall has a smell all of its own. The first frost brings a crispness to the air and reminds you to bring in more firewood. It's the time for county fairs, judging of livestock and can goods. We pause in November to give thanks and to celebrate with a feast of turkey and dressing and all the trimmings. We cut land and plant winter crops of wheat, oats, and rye. The garden is done except for harvesting sweet potatoes and turnip greens. Sorghum is gathered and made into syrup. Leaves are raked and burned as the days get shorter and shorter. Now is the season for hunting and spending wonderful afternoons following bird dogs. If the crops have been good we are excited about next year. If they have been bad we can always hope for better next year. As we lay down for sleep a quilt feels good and our minds turn to thoughts of repairs and rest.

 Winter brings on a time of peace and tranquility on the farm. It gives you time to rest, just as the earth you toil has to rest. All equipment, buildings, and fences are now being repaired. Christmas and New Year brings loved ones together for food and fun. There is something mystical and powerful about the first snow of the year. It's almost as if God is tucking the earth into bed after a long growing season. It's a time when we can see our breath steaming out in front of us. Farming is not an easy life, often times the stress seems unbearable, but the winter season gives us a time to draw closer to God and realize all our blessings come from Him. As we breath in the ice cold air and look at our land being nourished and replenished we are indeed thankful to be alive.

As the years come and go we will always have a springtime and a harvest time as long as the earth remains. Taking time to see our world up close lets us appreciate the gifts God gives us everyday.

A PERFECT LOVE

A church sign read, "A person can give without loving, but a person with love must give." As I thought about that slogan I thought about your mother, my wife. She is a truly remarkable woman that I fall in love with everyday. After we had finished dinner last night I was busy complaining about someone in the church being uncaring. As usual your mother stood up for the people and began to recite their good qualities. Your mom is inherently good. She can't find fault with anyone and is constantly trying to find good points about everyone. I guess if that is a fault it is a pretty good one to have. It is probably this quality that keeps her from having hurt feelings or carrying grudges.

In Matthew 5:24 we are told to…"first be reconciled to thy brother…" You know it's awful easy to love others on Valentines Day or Christmas but the rest of the time it becomes a chore. I find it so easy to love your mother, whether she is wearing an expensive evening gown or just a pair of jeans and a T-shirt, she is still the queen of my heart. Every time I look at you boys I believe that my heart is going to burst with the love I have for you. But these are my comfort zones when it comes to loving. Are we really expected to love the people that are difficult to love? Do we really have to love in-laws that treat us like outlaws? Do we really have to love those who have a different color skin or those who are poorer than we? Do we really have to love those who are not close to us? Your mother does!

Have you boys ever had someone to make you mad? Maybe they spoke harshly to you, or shunned you. Maybe your feelings are hurt. The best thing you can do for yourself is to go to that person with an outstretched hand and say, "Let's start over." You will be surprised at how great you feel. One of the greatest pleasures in life is to be "reconciled" with another human being. It's called never ending love, once you build a bridge for your love to pass, it also gives a way for their love to return. If we could all be more like your mother and love without condition we could stop a lot of problems before they start.

A SPECIAL LADY

Recollections of my childhood couldn't be complete without a very special lady in my life, my mother. Very few times in the course of a day goes by that I don't think of something my mother did for me. Your Maw-Maw Shinall has done many things right in her life, but being a mother certainly was best. It seemed while I was young that she did almost everything without effort, now that I'm a parent I know that wasn't the case at all.

Maybe now is a good time to take into account all the things that made my life much easier. I think of all the times she must have set up at night watching and worrying over me. How many nights did my coughing keep her up, or the nights she spent by my bed when I ran a fever. I remember once as a young boy having a terrific toothache and her rocking me all night. I am sure there were times as a teenager I must have made her stay awake with worry and fear. She had no problems scolding me when I had done wrong but always letting me know that she loved me.

My mother is the best cook in the world! It still amazes me that she can prepare a meal in a matter of minutes. Her Southern cooking can't be matched. She is an excellent baker, cooking cakes, cookies, pies, candy, and fresh baked bread. I can never remember many meals that were not followed by a wonderful desert. As a child I can remember her saying that a meal wasn't complete without at least one dessert. I will match her against any chef in the world today. She is magic at making leftovers into a feast.

I think of all the hours that she spent cleaning. Our home was always spotless, even when she was sick. She has never went to bed with a dirty dish in the house. Her washing and ironing could rival any modern laundry. Of course she didn't mind dusting my pants either! She always told me before every spanking that it hurt her more than it hurt me, often I thought that surely she must be dying!

As a child I was terrified of thunderstorms. Whenever one would come up at night she would always come and get in bed with me. Whenever I had a nightmare she would stay awake with me until I drifted back to sleep. What a special feeling it was for me to know that I had my own bodyguard.

She always nursed me back to health, Whether it was scratches, bruises, cuts, stitches, broken bones, flu, colds, allergies, bellyaches, or bites. She always gave good advice like, "Boy put on clean underwear in case your in an accident."

She taught me how to love animals, she loves them all. She fed every dog that I drug home. She never turned away an animal without trying to help it. She also helped me get over puppy love and assured me that someday I would have a very special lady come into my life.

Mother had a way with entertainment. Any birthday was celebrated with a feast. Thanksgiving, Christmas, New

Years, Fourth of July, and Easter were all celebrated in such a way that a young boy couldn't hardly wait for the next holiday. She made summertime cookouts fun and exciting. She did all this on a very limited budget.

She helped instill in me the belief that I could do anything that I wanted and become anything that I wanted to become. She built confidence in my life that has sure come in handy as I've gotten older. When it seemed like all hope was gone, she assured me that it wasn't. She kept the family together through thick and thin. And she made me realize that I always had a home to come back to and share with all my friends.

I remember the Christmas that I wanted a hunting knife. Mother had wrapped the knife but didn't realize that she had accidentally wrapped it with another gift. After searching the house frantically she cried herself to sleep Christmas Eve thinking I would be disappointed. I think of the times she needed a new dress but bought me clothes instead. I remember when there was four hungry people and only three pieces of pie, that she suddenly really didn't like pie any more.

Yes all these things and many, many more have created a treasure chest of memories for your dad. Many sweet precious hours of love went into raising me and for that I am most thankful. Anybody can become a mother, only a few become a mom.

Chapter 7
ARE YOU WILLING TO CHANGE?

Our lives are made up of continually changing situations. All too often we make any transition in our life a hassle. Statistics show that about thirty-five percent of all Americans die before they reach the age of sixty-five, fifty-five percent are broke at that age, they are forced to live in nursing homes or with their children. I couldn't imagine living with you boys after the way I've treated you! About five percent are still working at the age of sixty-five because they can't live off of social security. Four percent are self sufficient, they can live off of their savings and retirement, and only one percent will be rich. These are scary figures but I'd say they were pretty accurate.

What made the one percent succeed? It's probably due in most part because they weren't afraid to change or if they were afraid they changed anyway. Becoming successful will probably mean you will have to change your attitude. The only thing that sets a man apart from a horse is his mind. We have the ability to decide what our attitude will be. If you think you can do something you are right. If you think you can't do something you are right. The only difference between a millionaire and a pauper is their attitude.

We will have to start dreaming again. We will have to get a gut burning desire to see our lives improve if we are to be one of the success stories. As children we have no problems dreaming of success, we were always the hero, we never played bankruptcy or foreclosure, we dreamed big dreams. But as adults we get into what we call a routine, which is no more that a rut, which is no more than a grave with both ends knocked out.

In order to keep from being in the top ninety-five percent of the people at the age of sixty-five we might have to change what we are doing for a living. We might have to do some things that are uncomfortable. We might have to do some things that others refuse to do. The key is not to balk at change, it's often the only way God has of getting us to change directions.

"TOO SOON"
As I write this letter to you boys you are both very young and do all the things that seem to aggravate parents to no end. A dear friend of mine, who is a very sought after speaker, always ends his speeches with the following verses. I don't know who wrote it or who the credit goes to, I just know that it says something really special to all of us who call ourselves parents.

One of these days you'll shout why don't you kids grow up, and act your age! And they will. Why don't you kids get outside and find something to do, and don't slam the door! And they will. You'll straighten up the boys bedroom neat and tidy, toys displayed on the shelf and hangers in the closet, and you'll say out loud, I want it to stay this way! And it will. You'll prepare a perfect dinner with a salad that hasn't been picked to death and a cake with no finger traces on the icing and you say now there is a meal for company and you'll eat it alone. And you'll say I want complete privacy on the phone, no panamining going on behind me, no demolition crews, silence do you hear! And you'll have it. No more plastic table clothes stained with spaghetti, no more bed spreads to protect the sofa from wet bottoms. No more stumbling over toys. No more playpens to arrange a room around. No more sand on the sheets or toys in the bathtub. No more iron-on patches or wet knotted shoe strings, tight boots or rubber bands for pony tails. Imagine a lipstick with a point on it. No baby sitter to find and washing only once a week. And eating steak that isn't ground. Having your teeth cleaned without a baby in your lap. No more P.T.A. meetings, car pools, or blaring stereos. No one washing their hair in the middle of the night and having your own roll of tape.

Think about it, no more Christmas presents out of toothpicks and library paste. No more sloppy oatmeal kisses. No more tooth fairies. No more giggles in the dark or mommy I want a drink of water. No knees to heal and no responsibility.

Only a voice crying, "Why don't you grow up!" And the silence echoing back...I did.

Maybe I should make a few changes as a parent. I believe I will start with a new prayer.

"Father, teach me that I should always show love and understanding to my boys. Let me be a friend to my children instead of just a parent. Teach me to be more patient with their needs, because one day they won't need me at all."

THE DECISION

Well fellows it's been one of those days! It seems the harder I've worked the farther behind I've gotten, I'm right back to where I started from this morning. There was a time in my life when days like today infuriated me and made a restful nights sleep almost impossible, that's before I started letting everyday stand for itself.

There comes a time in everyone's life when he or she has to decide what they are going to do with God once they have found Him. I'm not talking about salvation, I'm talking about whether you live for Him fully or are you going to continue to straddle the fence. As I have often shared with you, I was saved at an early age and thought of myself as a very good Christian, however I never turned my business life over to God. I would go to church on Sundays, both morning and evening service. I taught Sunday school, I sang in the choir, but I refused to turn the reigns of my business over to God. I would make decisions day in and day out without ever consulting Him. I would spend thousands of dollars in my business and never seek His counsel on the direction I should take. Oh I was quick to beg for help when I got into trouble, but I really didn't think God knew much about running a business.

I remember well the Spring day I made my decision to let God rule and reign in all areas of my life. For several weeks I had been feeling God tugging at me about my life. I was very sure of my salvation, so I knew He was wanting me to do something more. I was cutting land one day in a thirty acre field, my mind was running like a computer. What could God possibly be wanting? Didn't I read my Bible and pray daily? What more could He want? Then God seemed to say, "Barry I want all of your life. Let me have control. You can't take all the time, you must learn to give."

The more I thought about it the more excited I got. I was forced to take an honest look at myself and it wasn't very pretty. I wanted so much to impress my family and friends with my success. I wanted my wife to be proud of me. Up until now I had not done a very good job.

Again God seemed to be speaking to me, "Do you trust me?"

"You know I trust you God!"

"Do you trust me enough to let me run your business and your life?"

I didn't know what to do. I was a serious Christian, but could I really go this far? Could I rely on God as a business partner? I also realized that if I did I could no longer take credit for all of my success. But wait, had I ever done anything all on my own? Of course not, He is always desiring to help us in every way.

I stopped the tractor in the middle of the field and laid my head on the steering wheel.

"Lord," I prayed out loud, "if this is what you want me to do, I'm willing. Take my life, all of it, business, personal, spiritual, and lead me. I promise I will be faithful to follow."

A new wave of assurance came over me. I felt like a million dollars! Although all of my business problems still existed, I felt assured they would be resolved now that I had made God C.E.O.

Has my life been full of exciting victories since then? Far from it, I have had to face many test, some of them painful. But I learn from all experiences and have found that if it is pushed it is from man, if it flows it is from God. We must not rely on our own self assurances but rather place our confidence in Him. Often I will spend hours in His word and in prayer to find the solution to a specific problem. Many times He will send other godly men to my rescue with their wisdom.

In Ecclesiastes 3:1-4 we are told that there comes a time for everything. Your time for the "Decision" will come. It might be while your young or after many years of life, but you will have to decide. I pray you boys make the right decision. Praise God from whom all blessings flow!

IN HIS SERVICE

I begin this writing to you boys, not to draw any attention to myself but to my Lord and Saviour Jesus Christ. I have hesitated to write this letter in fear that you boys might start thinking that I'm something more than I am. You know full well my feelings of religion and theology. You know about my salvation and my struggles to stay in Gods will. I would like to take this opportunity to share with you a turning point in my life that was difficult to accept and still provides its share of obstacles in my life.

I began to start feeling that God had a very special purpose for my life and I battled it every morning when I rose. I prayed and prayed for His guidance but found none. Before I go much farther let me emphasize that our timetable and Gods is not always the same. Different crop seeds take different amounts of time to mature, so it is with our prayers, the answer may not be immediate. I began to think God had called me into the ministry, actually I was relieved, since my early teens I had dreamed of being a preacher. I admire pastors so much in their roles of leaders and teachers. I had often thought of how nice it would be to spend your life as one of God's shepherds. So I began to pray in that direction, but with no success in easing my frustrations. I became depressed and felt like a thoroughbred race horse with no place to run. I fidgeted at my work and kicked the cat every time she would come around. Your mother and I attended a business seminar in St. Louis, against my will. I didn't want to go, but at the persistence of your mother and the Holy Spirit, I relented.

The weekend had been aggravating to me. The speakers were good but couldn't hold my interest. I would sneak up to my room and read my Bible but still I could find no answers to my dilemma. I prayed fervently for God to direct me, what ever it was, I was willing to do it. After getting terribly bored at one afternoon session I left the meeting room for a stroll in the lobby. As I walked I literally bumped into a fellow who introduced himself as Peter

Daniels. Immediately I was drawn to this man who spoke with an Australian accent. I remembered that he was to be one of our speakers that evening but I had never really heard of him before. After a few minutes of casual conversation, I ask what his topic would be when he spoke later on that night. His reply was to simply share his testimony of what God had done for him. As we found a seat he graciously shared with me how he had been an illiterate adult going no where when God told him that he had to become rich and serve Him. Through many struggles he became, almost miraculously, one of the richest, if not the richest, men in Australia. Now he shares his wealth generously for Gods work and shares his testimony all over the world. Immediately a great burden was lifted from me. Could this be what God wanted me to do? Simply be an obedient layman? It sounded so boring.

I went back into the meeting feeling much better but also somewhat scared. I had made God a promise, I told Him that if He would reveal his will I would do it. I had to be sure. I prayed often the next couple of days and told your mother on the way home of God's desire for my life. I told her that I felt God wanted me to be the best, most successful businessman I possibly could, and share with others that a Christian could be successful in business without all the vices portrayed on TV and the movies. This situation posed a few problems for me. First I wasn't even remotely successful, in order to have much of an impact on the world I would have to strive harder than ever before. A man who has never experienced the highs and lows of the business world could not give a very effective testimony to the business people he spoke to. Also I'm not particularly fond of crowds, they scare me. And I always thought of laymen as somewhat of an oddity. Many pastors I know don't take laymen very seriously, others respect them less. However, if this is what God wanted I was willing to give it a shot.

Since that time I've started enjoying life better than ever before. Sure the struggles for success in the business world are tough and frustrating, but with God as your C.E.O. it becomes easier. I've had the privilege of speaking before civic clubs, farm groups, churches, business seminars, and corporations. I still get scared before every speech, but soon after I start sharing with others about our victories through Christ, I relax and actually start enjoying myself. I have had the honor of personal witness and always want others to see Christ in me.

Often we have to do things that are uncomfortable. But I can not over emphasize the importance of obedience. Only then can we be sure of God's blessings.

CHINESE FOOD

As a boy growing up in a small Southern town, going out to eat was a great treat. Much of the time it was only for burgers and fries at the local greasy spoon, occasionally after church on Sunday we would go to the local diner for the blue plate special. I had never tried many fancy restaurants until I was grown, so knowing what to do was often difficult and awkward. Going to school I often carried biscuits and fried ham or sausage, home made pies or cake, while other children had sandwiches made from store bought bread and chips, boy did I envy them! Little did I realize at the time that mine was far superior to theirs.

After having done some lobbying at the state level, then on to the nation's capital, I became quite comfortable in even the ritziest of restaurants. As a lobbiest part of your duties were to entertain officials at dinner (still is supper to me). Many a vote has been persuaded over a fine cut of meat. While on a trip to Washington it fell my duty to take a distinguished Congressman out to dinner. Three of us from Georgia met our guest in the rotunda of the capital, after several minutes of polite chatter, we turned our conversation to where we would dine. Much to my dismay our guest wanted to eat Chinese food! I had never been in a Chinese restaurant, much less eaten any of their food. I am basically a meat and potatoes man, vegetables are great, casseroles OK, but stuff I don't recognize I had problems with.

We entered the restaurant only a few blocks away and immediately I knew that I was out of place. It was dark and the air smelled funny. This beautiful oriental girl ask us to remove our shoes! I couldn't believe my ears! Us men often have holes in our socks and you never know if your feet might offend someone, if you know what I mean?

We were seated at this little short legged table. We had to sit on the floor! This place didn't even own a chair. Now I like to be comfortable when I eat, a man of my posture can not be comfortable in the floor. The menu was passed around and I was completely lost. I didn't recognize a single dish. I figured that I would be safe if I ordered what the Congressman next to me ordered, so when ask what I wanted? I responded with, "I'll have the same!"

The conversation was on farm policy, but my mind was on the cuisine. I just couldn't figure out what I had ordered, and to be perfectly honest I was a little scared. Nevertheless my appetite was hearty so I waited patiently on my meal. In a few minutes they came out with this salad that was made of...bean sprouts! Man I dug those things out of the bottom of a combine, I wasn't about to eat them! Next came the soup, cold cucumber, it looked different, it tasted worst. The tea was green! Finally they brought out a thing that looked like a long biscuit, only crunchy, that was stuffed with something, it ate all right but I sure was hungry. I think my comrades could sense that I was out of place, but the communication was lively, and what the heck, I was getting paid to be there. After several minutes a little bitty bowl was placed next to my plate, I picked it up and smelled of it. It smelled like lemons but I decided against drinking it. Then the waiter placed a plate directly in front of me that had this long roll on it that was giving off steam. I was sure that it was our entree, but was it all mine or was I to share? I took up my fork and poked it, it was soft and pliable and I felt sure that it must be stuffed with something. After much consideration I decided that I should slice me off a piece and put it in my plate, then if they brought the others one I would know that this one was all mine, if not I guess I would have to share. Just as I picked up my knife and fork, I could sense everyone looking at me, oh well maybe they didn't want me to take too much. As my knife touched the roll, my distinguished, honorable, important guest poked me in the side and said, "Son, don't cut that napkin!"

 I thought that I would die! I was so embarrassed, I could see my whole career going down the drain. The table crowd broke into a horrendous laughter that drew the attention of every other person in the restaurant. The Congressman was quick to let everyone, who was anyone on Capital hill, know about my mistake. People would ask me how I liked my napkins, rare or well done? For days after at every meal someone would put a napkin in my plate. Even on the way home, the airline stewardess served everyone else their meal, to me she gave a rolled up napkin with a cherry on top!

 Boys, since that time I have fine tuned my eating habits. I now love Chinese food and eat it often. Changing can be very difficult at times!

"WHAT IF"

It seems to me that one thing that often disrupts our peace of mind is finances. So many people, including myself, have had many struggles with this area of life, and one reason for the lack of money is being afraid to step out. Many times a new job offer will come along or the opportunity arises to start a business of your own and we become paralyzed with fears. We find many excuses for imagined security, effort already put forth, benefits, that our current situation provides. What it all boils down to is that we just don't like making the change. Well if you boys ever find yourselves in this predicament I hope I can help.

Millions of people find themselves in jobs or business' that are not providing for their families finances adequately. I like the old saying, "If the horse is dead, take the saddle off!" I have talked to many people who need extra income but are unwilling to do anything about it. Often they love what they are doing but are not getting ahead, or in many cases not even keeping up! A great friend of mine once told me that a good businessman must not think with his heart; but rather with his head. That is sound advice. Sure it's hard to do something that is different than your chosen profession, but often it may be necessary. I don't know what keeps people that hate what they do from changing, but many refuse to even discuss other avenues of financial achievement.

A sharp Christian businessman once gave me a formula of questions that he called the "What If's." Only four questions, but all very important, if your thinking about making a business decision. After using these questions in hundreds of different situations, I would like to apply them to the need of changing your financial outlook.

(1) What if this new business is only half as good as I believe it to be? Well take the best case scenario, and cut it in half. Does it still look good or even acceptable? Most people like to overestimate, this gives you a more humbling viewpoint. However if this new income still looks good at only half of what you think it could be, then it is probably a real good decision. Don't forget, often a second job, or even an "on the sides' business, can literally change your finances overnight. (2) What if this new business takes me a long time to succeed? Could I answer that with another question? How fast are you succeeding now? I once knew a man who had worked at the same place for eighteen years and was barely getting by. After looking at a great business opportunity his reply was, "This thing might take me five years to put together!" I couldn't believe my ears! Here was a man who had given his life to someone else and wasn't making ends meet, but he was afraid to give five years to himself for what looked like a good opportunity. (3) What if this new business doesn't work? This question is only important if your already doing well financially. You see, if your not making it now and you try something else then you haven't lost anything. Let me caution you here, never, ever, gamble money you don't have! Not on a new business. Not on the Stock Market. Not on the farm. Look at the situation. If you can survive the loss of your investment over the next two or three years, then you are probably in safe territory, if not seek out a professionals opinion before making any changes. About the only thing most of us have to invest is time and money, true both are precious commodities, but if your needing more of both, then maybe a change in performance is just what's needed. (4) What if this new business does work, but I reject it? Ahh! This question is usually never asked. Most people today will only glance at

opportunity and never give any serious thought as to what might have been if they had acted. This really came home to me a few years ago. A friend, who was also a farmer, came by in 1982 with a new business fresh under his wing. He felt sure that we both could get rich and he was excited! After looking at what he was doing, I wanted to get excited, but status wouldn't let me. Status is when you have a title and no money. Well you guessed it, I turned him down. When I was forced to sell my home to pay bills, he was buying a condo in Gulf Shores. When I was forced to sell my car to pay bills, he was buying a new Mercedes. When I became a farm manager for someone else, he was hiring a farm manager to run his operation. Yes boys you're right, I wanted to throw up!

Of course never make any major decision without first praying about it and giving it ample thought. Consult your spouse and seek the counsel of God fearing men. Another word of caution, never go around asking everybody and anybody's opinion about your future. If they haven't given sufficient prayer and research into your situation, they very well could steer you wrong. When I decided that I wanted to grow corn, I didn't ask the guy at the service station how to do it! I ask the farmer who had always had success in growing corn! Remember fellows, life is not a dress rehearsal, we only have one shot to make this one great!

A HEAVY HEART

As I write this letter to you boys, my heart is heavy and my throat seems tight. It is very late and very quiet here in our beloved farm home. I hear the wind blow outside my office window while you and your mother are bound by restful sleep. The weather is unusually warm for February, and predictions for rain are high.

Late this afternoon my mother, your grandmother, called and told me that one of my uncles had suddenly taken ill at work and had been rushed to the local hospital. Only a few minutes had passed when I arrived at the local hospital emergency room to find your mother and another aunt already there. They gave me the tragic news that he had died of a massive heart attack only moments before. He was forty-three years old. He left behind a wife and five children. Two things that bother your dad is to hear babies cry and to see good men die. Oh, I realize that death is just as much a part of life as birth and it is assigned unto everyone a time to die, but that doesn't mean that accepting it is always easy.

After a few minutes of discussion it was decided that an aunt and myself would go tell the children and his mother that their dad and her son was dead. Now boys I've done a lot of hard things in my life, some very unpleasant, but none worse than what my duty was today. It's so hard for us to lose a mate or a child or a brother but none can compare to the grief of a young child who only an hour ago had a father, only now to have a dark, vast, void. Now they have no dad to turn to when they need help. No special dad to share those precious moments of a growing child. The screams of pain, the moans of agony, the sobs of grief, all came this afternoon as the news was revealed. The kids needed someone to be strong, and so I was. Not a tear fell from my eyes as I held jerking shoulders and kissed foreheads. I reassured them that the passing of time would help heal their tragically torn hearts. I prayed for comfort and guidance. I prayed for strength to endure the coming days. Soon many loving family members were there, how fortunate to have friends and family at a time like this.

As I sit at my desk and write this evening, I let my tears flow freely. I don't begrudge death, we serve a merciful

God who prepares a place for those that believe in Him. But the faces of those young children will never escape me. The change that occurred in their lives today is irreversible, it was also unwanted. You see fellows, not all change is elected. Many things come into our lives that will make a drastic change in our lifestyles, but only *you* can determine how they will effect you. You can let unwanted changes destroy your life and make you miserable, or you can use them to unlock unknown doors of opportunity. What will happen to the kids? Where will they go? What will they do? I don't know. Only the fleeing of time can answer these questions and determine how an untimely change will effect them on life's wayward journey.

THE TEACHER

Teachers come in many shapes, colors, and ages. They may teach you in class or in Sunday School. They may teach you from a pulpit or from grandma's rocker. Whatever the situation, many people will come into our lives who will help to shape us into who we are, often it is a thankless job, all too often we push their memories onto the back porches of our minds. I have several fond memories of several teachers in my life, but my favorite teacher of all time was a college professor by the name of O'Mary.

He had a tremendously successful career in the agricultural and education field. Now in the twilight of his career he was the head of the Ag department at a small north Georgia school. His achievements in his chosen field had been numerous and impressive, but now he seemed content to end his career doing what was his first love, teaching young men and women. His knowledge of agriculture was phenomenal, he would forget more about the subject than I would ever learn. But not only did he do a superb job in the classroom, he spent many hours of his personal time helping young adults with their intricate problems. He was a comforter to those who were homesick, he was a witness to those who didn't know Christ as their personal Saviour. He set a great example to those around him as how a responsible adult should act.

My last visit with the old scholar has been a valuable asset to my life. The setting was at the beautiful college campus at Mt. Berry, Georgia. It was a rainy Spring afternoon, and as was his custom, he was treating his class to an "all you can eat" steak cookout, at the end of the semester. There was much laughter and excitement as freshmen and seniors alike were enjoying the festivities. I found Dr. O'Mary alone enjoying a prime cut of meat and watching "his kids" have a good time. I ask if I could eat with him and was warmly welcomed to his table. As we talked of farming and techniques, his conversation turned to more somber thoughts of his beloved deceased wife and the end of his career.

I had the wonderful privilege that day of sharing my dreams with my old friend. I ask his opinion on what I should do to become the very best farmer possible.

"Well," he said, "if there is one thing that I can call my own, it is my opinions. Advice is cheap, and what I can tell you about life is only what I know works for me."

For the next hour he shared with me those precious little jewels that I scratched down on a napkin.

He told me that a person should always be *Patient*. If a person is impatient he will spend much of his time worrying over things that are worthless. The man who realizes that every job is worth doing right, is the man who can look back on his labors at the end of the day and be proud. The same could be said about careers. He said that the successful farmer is the one willing to wait for his efforts to mature and not try to hurry nature along. The man who looses his temper is a man who can not control his emotions. The man who can not control his emotions is out of control and will eventually crash.

He told me that we should be *happy*. This may be the hardest of all things to do. So many times in our lives it seems almost impossible to be happy. However, the world needs people who will make others feel warm and appreciated. It is the happy man who will dry the tears of those who cry. It is the happy person who has an abundance of friends. It is the happy people who help mend broken spirits. Although it may be hard to be continuously happy, those that do will lead a richer more rewarding life.

He told me that we need people today that will tell the *truth*. Honesty is the best policy, but it is the policy that most people never adhere to. Men need to be willing to let their word be their bond. A lie is a lie, no big ones, no little ones, just all corruptible and disgraceful. Every time that a man lies it destroys his character bit by bit. A mans character is all he has when he doesn't have anything else.

He told me that I should always *love my country*. A man needs to be ready to die for it if the need ever arises.

We have a great privilege to live and farm in this land of the free, let's never take it for granted. While others find fault with our land we need to be fiercely loyal to the Red, White, and Blue. A man who is not patriotic is a man you can not trust.

He told me that we should *always keep learning*. Our mind is a great asset that too many people waste. The farmer who quits expanding his knowledge will eventually be out of business. A person is never too old to improve his mind. He should never be too busy to enhance his education. A man who keeps up with life will never be left behind.

He told me to always be *brave*. Men should be men and quit trying to hide behind others. Too many men today are afraid to face life head-on. They rely on their wives to run the house, pay the bills, and discipline the kids. A man should zip his britches up the front and meet his problems rather that run from them. If this country had more brave men we would have a stronger society in which to live. Everyday new dragons will raise their ugly heads and it is up to the brave men to slay them. Give your kids something they can be proud of, a brave daddy.

Last but not least, he told me to *always do what YOU enjoy doing*. Life is so short, we try so hard to make a living, that we forget how to make a life. Take time to stop and smell the roses, they will only bloom for a while, then they are gone. The saddest of all men is the man who looks back at life's end and wishes for what it might have been. A person should be able to make a living doing what he enjoys, if he will apply success principles to his life. Don't be afraid of work, it's what will eventually make your achievements. The worst parasite on earth is the man who refuses to earn his keep.

As the rain ended and the party broke up, I stood and shook hands with the professor. Not only had he taught me much about my chosen field of endeavor, he had shared with me things that would make my life better. Here I was beginning my career, he was finishing his. Changes, life is full of them, one life begins another ends. As you boys go through life try to apply these principles to your own lives. They will not make you a success, but they will make you a better man.

At the time of this writing my old friend is living in his native Alabama, enjoying retirement with a wonderful new wife. We have kept in touch by phone and Christmas cards but I don't think he will ever know what he means to me. A teacher taught, a student listened.

Chapter 8

WHAT'S NEXT?

It has been several months since I've written to you boys in this journal. Many exciting things have been taking place in my life. I've started a new business venture with my mentor, Ken. I've just finished planting which has taken many days of hard toil but has given much pleasure. Officially this is my sixteenth crop and I'm just as excited today as I was sixteen years ago. Just this morning I went out to survey the fields and found tender young vegetation already springing forth from God's good earth.

As I sit in the upstairs hallway, which is actually much larger than the first living room your mother and I had, I am taking a few minutes to rest after many days of constant work. I settle into the comfortable blue armchair, light my pipe and begin reading a good book. In no time at all Matt is in my lap busily trying to catch the smoke from the pipe. He laughs and giggles as he vainly tries to catch the allusive prey, oh he can push it one way or the other. He can determine the direction that the smoke travels, but he can never, as hard as he might try, harness it. That's a lot like life itself, this is not a dress rehearsal, it's the real thing. We vainly try to master it and then sooner or later the fire will go out and the game will be over.

I must now turn to the task of bringing this journal to a close. There are so many more stories to tell, more lessons to teach, more love to share, but for the time being I must somehow find a place to stop. No matter how good the play might be, the most dedicated playgoer would soon get bored if the play never ended.

THUMBS UP

In many ways the farm is much like a community. There seems to be an endless variety of tasks to fill the days, many people and animals working hard together, children laughing, things dying, and lots and lots of sweet memories. As I write this I find myself again far from home, in a big city hotel room, far from you boys and your dear mother. Often my heart gets heavy and I fear it will break from missing my old life so. Now because of economic reasons beyond my control I, like so many others, must make a living away from our farms. Oh I'm not complaining, God has given me a great opportunity to help others, but still I get very homesick for the life that I loved for so long. It is times like this when I like to recall some of those wonderful, funny events that happened on the farm and still make me laugh when they come unbidden to my mind. Let me share a couple of them now with you boys.

Your "Uncle Horace," who is actually my uncle, thus a great uncle to you boys, and I have been farming together since I was your age Tom. As a small boy I would ride for hours unending on the tractor with uncle Horace. He knew then how much I loved the land. He also knew that I loved him and I knew he loved me, and thus a partnership was formed that has lasted nearly thirty years. Uncle Horace has always loved a good joke and has pulled more than one "good-one" in his day, however, one Spring I had the privilege of getting-one on him.

One of the farm hands and myself had planted most of the crop this particular year, and uncle Horace was beside himself with worry. He just knew that we would mess something up without him on the scene. Every so often he would come to the field in his old blue Chevy pickup to survey the disaster we must be making. Usually the seeds were either too shallow or too deep or just plain not right. On this warm Spring morning we had been making good time when he pulled into the field.

Sure enough out through the field he went digging here and there, looking for seed. Finally he stopped us and began adjusting the planter to his desired depth. During this time the tractor pulling the cutting harrow pulled along side of uncle Horace's truck and stopped so the man driving could get a drink of water. Looking at the cutting harrow a devilish thought jumped all over me.

The dust on top of the cutting harrow was about two inches thick and as fine as snuff. That gave me the idea. You see, uncle Horace dearly loves his snuff and is never without it. On this day his snuff can was on the dash of his pickup. So while uncle Horace worked on and swore at the planter, I took his snuff can and threw out the snuff, thus replacing it with field dust! After finishing his job he sauntered over to his truck, hitched up his overalls, and took him a big cud full of "snuff." I could hardly keep a straight face. Watching him work up that dirt in his mouth was nearly more than I could stand! Suddenly he began to speak, and little puffs of dust came from the corners of his mouth!

"Tis snuf tas jus lak curt!"

He spit a time or two, got in his truck and left with a mouth full of what he thought was the worst snuff he had ever tasted! I have not had the nerve to reveal this joke to uncle Horace to this day. Please boys, help me keep my secret!

Your mother has always had very expensive taste. Take her to a dress shop and she will invariably go to the most expensive thing in the whole store. Ever since I married your mother she has always wanted a two seater Mercedes sport car, she loves them.

One day I had gone to a farm auction in Cave Springs where I purchased a Mercedes Benz 1113, ten wheel, two ton truck. Since the day was getting late I decided to call home and let your mother know that I was going to be late. While speaking to her she ask if I had bought anything? I told her that as a matter of fact I had, I had bought a Mercedes! Well immediately she ask if it were a two seater? Well yes I said. She wanted to know what color? White I said.

"Is it a straight shift?" she ask.

"Yes it is." was my reply. I simply failed to tell her that it was a ten speed.

"Gas or diesel?" she ask.

"Diesel." said I. And I also told her that it had a sun roof, and it did!

"Honey take your time coming home because I'm going to fix your favorite supper!" she exclaimed as she hung up the phone.

I want you boys to notice that I never did tell a lie. I didn't tell her everything, but I didn't lie!

It was dark when I rolled up into the driveway in the big truck and as I pulled on the emergency brake and released the air pressure, I saw your mother bust through the front door onto the porch. She ran laughing and holding her hands until she got within ten feet of the truck and saw the Mercedes emblem on the front of the grill. She stopped dead still, turned, walked back to the house, and didn't speak for several days!

Well boys, the hour is late and my schedule is full for tomorrow, so I must quit telling tales for the time being. I want you both to know that daddy loves you both very much and I wouldn't change either of you if I could. I think you are perfect the way you are. If I could wish upon a star tonight, I wouldn't wish for anything more than what I have in you.

SOAR LIKE AN EAGLE

Don't stop and try to understand why I feel like a king on the throne tonight, it's not important. As I take pen in hand, I am miles away from my beloved North Georgia farm and the ones that I love. It's Fall now, my time of year. I sit here at the desk in my room, looking out the window at the beautiful North Carolina mountains. And even though it is dark, I can tell that the trees are a blaze of color. It is beginning to rain, I love the rain.

I never knew when or how I would end this journal until tonight. Now, although the hour is very late I realize that I must lay it to rest. I spend much of my time traveling now, doing meetings, training seminars, and public speaking. I fill my hours telling others how to be successful. How to overcome the adversities of life. How to survive and thrive. Yes my life is full of excitement and fulfillment. Yet it seems like only yesterday, as a teenager I would spend hours under the Georgia moon wishing I could be somebody. I really didn't know exactly what I wanted, I just wanted to make a difference in peoples lives. The road to where I'm at didn't come easy. It was filled with potholes and dangerous curves, yet that dream of breaking the chains that held me back was always there. After your mother and I were married, I would finish supper and tell your mother that I was going out for fresh air. I would take my old truck and my dog, drive to some deserted place on the farm and park. I would climb in the back of the truck and spend hours looking at the sky and dreaming. Dreaming that one day I would amount to something. Dreaming that someday after wading through all the muck and mire that somehow I would reach the shores of success. Often I wanted it so bad I would cry. No one was there to see me but the dog and God. I would pray and cry and wish for a more meaningful life, only to return to my 60 foot by 12 foot trailer and reality.

I had no idea that God was answering my prayers. It would be years before I became a public speaker. I had to learn from painful, personal experiences, so that I might be better able to help others. I still find it hard to believe that folks would come from miles around to hear your daddy speak. Tonight a young man came up to me to express his feelings. He really didn't have to say anything, I could see it in his eyes. I could see what you see in any high achiever, a dream. He told me how hard he was struggling to make a living for him and his young family. He assured me that one day he would succeed. That his financial bondage would be broken, and that his life would be as exciting as mine. With a smile on my lips and joy in my heart, I hugged him and assured him that I believed he could do it!

Tonight I realize that success isn't measured by money, reputation, or power, yet it is the love of a family like ours. It's the companionship of a woman like your mother. It's making a commitment to your dreams, not someone else's. I guess these reasons must have been there all along, only now do I realize their power.

I will be home in a few days and you boys will run to greet me. You will climb in my lap and cover me with peanut butter kisses. You will ask me what type people did I meet? And I will answer by telling you that I was with a bunch of winners! It's good to know that there are still those around with a dream in their heart and a hope in their mind that someday, somehow, their goals will be reached. Bet what you want to on it, they are the ones that will one day rise up and soar like and eagle.

EPILOGUE

One of my hero's is Lt. Clebe McClary, wounded Vietnam veteran, evangelist, and motivational speaker. Clebe recites a poem called *A Careful Marine*. I want to substitute Farmer for Marine in honor of you boys.

> A careful farmer I want to be
> for little fellows follow me.
> I do not care to go astray,
> for fear they may go the selfsame way.
> I can not once escape their eye,
> what e'er they see me do they'll try.
> Like me they say their going to be,
> those little lads who follow me.
> They think that I am big and fine,
> believe in every word of mine.
> The base in me they must not see,
> those little lads who follow me.
> I must remember as I go through Summer
> suns and Winter snows.
> I'm building for the years to be
> those little lads who follow me.

Daddy loves you!